HEAVEN CAN WAIT

★

COMEDY-FANTASY IN THREE ACTS

BY HARRY SEGALL

★

DRAMATISTS
PLAY SERVICE
INC.

CAST OF CHARACTERS

Principal Characters:

Joe Pendleton
Mr. Jordan
Messenger 7013
Julia Farnsworth
Tony Abbott
Bette Logan
Max Levene

Minor Characters:

Mrs. Ames
Nurse
Susie, Maid
Ann, Maid
Williams
First Escort
Second Escort
Workman
Lefty
Doctor
Plainclothesman

Extras: Non-speaking parts for airplane passengers, members of crowd, trainers, messengers, etc.

SYNOPSIS OF SCENES

ACT I

SCENE 1: Corner of a flying field.

SCENE 2: The Farnsworth living-room.

ACT II

SCENE 1: The same, next morning.

SCENE 2: Same, three weeks later.

ACT III

SCENE 1: The same, a week later.

SCENE 2: Dressing-room underneath
Stadium, immediately after.

NOTE: The principal set is the Farnsworth living-room described on page 16. The corner of a flying field (Act I, Scene 1) requires practically no scenery and no furniture. Act III, Scene 2, is the corner of a dressing-room in which only a bare wooden table and a couple of chairs are required. Each of these scenes is described in its proper place.

HEAVEN CAN WAIT

ACT I

SCENE I: *A brilliant, warm, sun-drenched flying field upon which stands a fairly large passenger plane, almost ready to take off.*

The above description of the set represents what may be used if the director so desires. However, it is suggested that this scene be played against a neutral undecorated backdrop and that the airplane be considered as off-stage, either R. *or* L. *Possibly the end of the steps leading to the door of the plane might be shown. The set can be very shallow and the scene might even be played before the stage curtain. The number of non-speaking parts can be expanded or reduced.*

AT RISE. *A diversified group of* PASSENGERS: *male, female, old, young, white, colored, of various creeds—all in charge of an* ESCORT (*1st Escort*) *in flying uniform, are entering plane. Some are gay, some sad, some introspective—a mingling of moods one would find in almost any group leaving on some journey—with this significant difference: there are no friends or relatives to see them off, to wave them goodbye. At* L. *and* R. *stand similar* GROUPS, *also in charge of* ESCORTS, *waiting for first group to enter plane.*

Standing by steps leading into plane is MR. JORDAN, *the Pilot, a rugged, rosy-cheeked, rather testy old fellow in blue aviation uniform, checking in the passengers. As the uniformed* 1ST ESCORT *calls off names,* JORDAN *scans his list, checks names, and* PASSENGERS *enter the plane. It is all quite business-like and systematic.*

1ST ESCORT. (*Calls.*) Gaylow, William.
JORDAN. (*Scans list, mumbling the name.*) Gaylow, Gaylow, Gaylow —— (*Puts check-mark opposite name and calls.*) Check.

5

(PASSENGER *named* GAYLOW *enters plane.*)

1ST ESCORT. Zabel, Frederick.

JORDAN. (*Testily.*) Zabel, that's Z. You're leaping from G to Z. Haven't you anyone between those letters?

1ST ESCORT. (*Respectfully.*) Yes, sir.

JORDAN. (*Snaps.*) Well, then, call them off alphabetically. You've been at this long enough to know the rules.

1ST ESCORT. (*Humbly.*) Yes, sir. My mistake. Sorry, sir.

JORDAN. Continue.

1ST ESCORT. Heggie, Alicia.

JORDAN. Heggie, Heggie —— (*Sees name.*) Check.

(MISS HEGGIE *enters plane.*)

1ST ESCORT. Ingle, Peter.

JORDAN. Ingle—check.

1ST ESCORT. Irwin, Lucy.

JORDAN. Irwin—check. (*To* 1ST ESCORT *as* IRWIN *enters plane.*) That's better—saves a lot of work.

1ST ESCORT. Yes, sir. Jacobson, Morris.

JORDAN. Jacobson—check.

(JACOBSON *enters plane.*)

1ST ESCORT. Washington, Hannah.

JORDAN. Nothing between Jacobson and Washington?

1ST ESCORT. No, sir.

JORDAN. Washington, Washington—check.

(MISS WASHINGTON, *colored, enters plane.*)

1ST ESCORT. Zabel, Frederick.

JORDAN. Zabel—check.

(ZABEL *enters plane.*)

1ST ESCORT. That is all, sir. (*He salutes* JORDAN *and follows after* ZABEL.)

JORDAN. (*Mops brow and calls out to* 2ND ESCORT *at* R.) All right— you're next.

2ND ESCORT. (*To his group.*) Attention. This way, please. (*He conducts them near plane and salutes* JORDAN.) Messenger 3081 reporting, sir. Five passengers.

JORDAN. Territory?

2ND ESCORT. The Southeast of Finland.

JORDAN. (*Makes note on list and grunts.*) Proceed—alphabetically, mind you.

2ND ESCORT. Yes, sir. (*Calls.*) Abilius, William.

JORDAN. Abilius, Abilius—check.

(ABILIUS *enters plane.*)

2ND ESCORT. Kilija, George.

JORDAN. Kilija—check. (*As* KILIJA *enters plane,* TWO MALE VOICES *raised in heated argument heard off-stage. Annoyed.*) What in gracious heaven is that?

(*The owners of the* VOICES *enter—that is, one enters, the other is propelled in. The "propelled" one is* JOE PENDLETON, *a big, brawny, sweet but simple fellow about 24. He carries a saxophone which he hugs under his* L. *arm as though afraid it's going to be wrenched away from him. The "propeller" is another of the* ESCORTS—*Messenger 7013, to be exact—a slight, meticulous, precise, little man of about 50.*)

JOE. (*Lusty and angry.*) What is this? What am I doing up here? What's the matter with you guys—screwy or something?

7013. (*Refined, precise, but equally annoyed.*) I'm fast losing patience with you, Mr. Pendleton; resign yourself to the fact that you have nothing, absolutely *nothing,* to say in this matter.

JOE. (*Heatedly.*) Oh, is that so? (*Looks about and bellows angrily.*) Who's in charge around here? (*Grimly.*) I'll settle this thing quick!

7013. It's all settled as far as *you* are concerned, Mr. Pendleton, believe me.

JOE. Yeah? We'll see about that!

JORDAN. (*To* ESCORT *at plane.*) Excuse me. (*Comes down to* JOE *and* 7013; *gruffly.*) What's the trouble?

7013. (*Respectfully saluting.*) Messenger 7013 reporting. No trouble at all, sir.

JOE. Yes, there is—there's plenty of trouble—an' there's going to be a hulluva lot more if ——

7013. (*Sharply.*) Hush!

JOE. (*Angrily.*) I'm not hushing. I'm gonna squawk my head off. (*To* JORDAN.) Are you the boss?

7013. (*To* JOE; *sharply.*) A little more respect, Mr. Pendleton. This is *Mister Jordan!*

JOE. (*Quite unimpressed.*) Oh, it is, eh? Well, Mister Jordan, this

7

guy here —— (*Indicates* MESSENGER 7013.) —— *tells me I'm dead!*

7013. Take my word for it, Mr. Pendleton, you are most certainly dead, else I shouldn't have taken you.

JOE. That don't prove nothin'! You just plucked the wrong bird, pal! You fellas make mistakes too, you know!

7013. Mistakes? We? How utterly fantastic!

JOE. Look, a fella ought to know if he's dead or not, I guess.

7013. (*Turns to* JORDAN.) Pay no attention to him, sir. He's a very difficult case—fought me tooth and nail all the way up here!

JOE. I ain't started fightin' yet. If you guys think you can drag me ——

JORDAN. (*Sternly.*) Silence! (JOE *subsides; somehow he senses in* JORDAN *an authority not lightly disobeyed. To* 7013; *indicates* JOE.) Is he all you gathered?

7013. (*Timorously.*) Yes, sir. I'm sorry, sir.

JOE. You're going to be a lot sorrier.

7013. Oh, for heaven's sake, be still!

JORDAN. Who is he?

7013. Pendleton, Joseph.

JOE. You even got my name balled up—it's Joe Pendleton—not Pendleton Joseph.

(JORDAN *starts scanning list, mumbling "Pendleton, Pendleton, Pendleton"; turns a page.*)

JORDAN. (*To* 7013.) What territory do you cover? (*Continues looking.*)

7013. A place called New Jersey, sir, and if it can be arranged, I should very much like to be transferred.

(JORDAN *keeps scanning list, turning pages.*)

JOE. You won't find me on no list. Don't waste your time looking. I ain't ready for wherever you want to take me.

7013. You're bound for Heaven, Mr. Pendleton—you'll hear the inner music of the spheres; you'll walk upon the shores of the crystal sea; you'll watch the flowers break and blossom in the moonlight; you'll know a happiness beyond achievement in the world you just left; you'll reap the harvest after the famine and drought of mundane existence; you'll ——

JORDAN. (*Snaps.*) Stop selling him the place. Against the rules.

7013. Sorry, sir.

JOE. (*To* 7013.) Look, you're a nice little guy and I don't want to hurt your feelings, but honest, my number ain't up. It *can't* be.

JORDAN. (*Still mumbling.*) Pendleton, Pendleton, Pendleton —— (*Turns another page.*)

7013. (*Triumphantly to* JOE.) Oh, he'll find it, all right.

JOE. What'll you bet? (*Sticks hands in pockets, then with a start, quickly withdraws them and looks suspiciously at* 7013.) Hey, what did you do with my roll?

7013. You won't need any "roll" up here.

JORDAN. (*To* JOE.) What did you do? Your occupation?

JOE. (*Proudly.*) Me? I'm a pug—a fighter —— (*He "squares" off.*) You know. And when I ain't fightin' I'm flyin'. I do commercial flying for a firm in Jersey. McGovern, Rafferty & Blunt. Make two trips a week—Boston, Toledo, Chicago and Omaha—everybody knows me—the "Flyin' Fighter."

7013. (*Significantly.*) You *were* the Flying Fighter!

JOE. I still am!

JORDAN. (*To* 7013; *sharply.*) There's no Pendleton, Joseph listed.

JOE. (*Triumphantly to* 7013.) What'd I tell you, smart guy?

7013. (*Worried, to* JORDAN.) Are you quite certain, sir?

JORDAN. (*Snaps.*) The lists are infallible. (*Severely.*) You've made a mistake.

7013. (*To* JORDAN, *falteringly.*) A mistake? But that's not possible, sir.

JORDAN. (*Snaps.*) Why not?

7013. Why, I—I ——

JORDAN. You're *new*, aren't you?

7013. Yes, sir. I—I was put on only this morning. This is my first trip.

JORDAN. (*Grimly.*) I thought so. Over-zealousness; out for record collections; this happens right along with the inexperienced.

7013. (*Astonished.*) You actually mean, sir, that these—these *errors* are not infrequent? That we often collect souls before —— ?

JORDAN. That's precisely what I mean!

7013. (*Distressed.*) Oh, dear. Oh, dear me. I had no idea such a thing was possible. (*To* JOE.) I—I'm afraid I owe you an apology, Mr. Pendleton.

JOE. (*Good-naturedly.*) Aw, it's okay, Mister. No harm done. We all make mistakes! Just take me back and forget it.

7013. (*Gratefully.*) Thank you, Mr. Pendleton. You're a kindly spirit, but I'm afraid there's no taking you back.

JOE. Why not?

JORDAN. (*Peremptorily to* JOE *and* 7013.) Quiet! (*To* JOE.) How old are you?

JOE. Twenty-two—be twenty-three in April and "in the pink"!

JORDAN. (*Pointing to* JOE's *saxophone; to* 7013.) How did he manage to wangle that thing up here?

7013. I couldn't get him to leave it behind, sir.

JOE. (*Grins.*) I never let go of this. (*Pats saxophone lovingly.*) It's my buddy—keeps my lungs in shape. I take it up in the plane with me the mornings I make the trip—just when the sun's coming up. I set the controls for blind flyin', fill my lungs with all that sweet ozone, sit back and give out. Boy, you should hear me—up there, away from everything, I play things I never thought was in me! Levene says ——

JORDAN. Who is Levene?

JOE. My manager—he's got a piece of me—swell guy. Picked me up one night when he saw me put away "Butcher Boy" McKenzie in Astoria; told me I had "color"; I was what the fans wanted—you know, like the "Manassa Mauler."

JORDAN. (*To* 7013; *perplexed.*) What's he talking about?

7013. (*Shrugging.*) I really don't know, sir.

JORDAN. What is a Manassa Mauler?

JOE. (*Stares at them.*) Yuh kiddin'?

7013. We don't "kid," Mr. Pendleton.

JOE. You mean you two guys never heard of the Manassa Mauler? Of Dempsey?

JORDAN. Afraid not.

JOE. You don't get around much, do you? (*Sarcastically.*) I suppose you never heard of Rudy Vallee, either?

JORDAN. Is he another Manassa Mauler?

JOE. (*Grins.*) Now I know you're clownin'.

JORDAN. (*Signals to* ESCORT *standing near plane.* ESCORT *hurries over and touches his cap; to* ESCORT.) Ask the Registrar for the file on Pendleton, Joseph, and get me a copy of the *latest* listing.

ESCORT. Yes, sir. (*Touches cap and exits.*)

JORDAN. (*To* 7013.) There's a possibility he may be on the new list.

7013. Oh, I hope so, sir.

JOE. (*Angrily.*) Now, look here. Don't try to fenagle me on any list. I got my whole life to live yet. (*He struts his physical powers.*) I'm "in the pink," I tell you. I ain't ready for this joint yet.

7013. To what shining pleasures do you wish to return? The rush to catch a train? The enervating manna of the refrigerator and the tin? War, hatred, persecution—the rule of Might —— ?

JOE. (*Simply.*) Yeah, I know—the going gets pretty tough sometimes, but just the same it's lots of fun; fallin' in love, gettin' married; havin' kids; makin' somebody happy, being somebody. It's swell and I don't want to miss any part of it!

JORDAN. (*To 7013.*) How in Pandemonium did you happen to pick him up?

JOE. He caught me just as I was ——

7013. Please, Mr. Pendleton, this is strictly *my* domain. (*To* JORDAN.) It was like this, sir: I was on my way back to report a singularly fruitless day when I suddenly saw Mr. Pendleton's plane cracking up. I immediately hopped aboard and as we went plummeting earthward, his terror-stricken face turned upward in prayer, harrowed my very soul. (*Apologetically.*) Sir, I know we Messengers shouldn't permit our emotions to sway us, but I could spare him indescribable agony by simply taking him off with me *before* the plane actually crashed— and well, sir, forgive me, sir, that is exactly what I did.

JORDAN. Unpardonably presumptuous.

7013. (*Miserably.*) Yes, sir. I'm desolate about it, sir.

JOE. (*To 7013.*) Say, you're a pretty good skate, at that, and I appreciate what you tried to do, but just the same, I wouldn't have crashed. No, sir! I'd have got the ship under control somehow—something would have saved me. Nothing ever happens to me when I've got my lucky sax along.

7013. It's *impossible* you were spared. You were hurtling to earth with the speed of a meteor. You were probably smashed to bits— burned to a crisp as well.

JOE. (*Simply.*) No, it wasn't in the cards. I don't know why I'm so sure—I just feel it.

7013. (*Testily.*) You don't feel anything. You didn't feel the crash, did you?

JOE. No, but that's because I didn't crash.

7013. Next, you'll be telling me you weren't flying.

JOE. Oh, I was flyin', all right.

(*The* ESCORT *re-enters, comes up to* JORDAN *and hands him a sheaf of papers.*)

JORDAN. (*Taking them.*) We'll soon settle this. (ESCORT *returns to his place at plane while* JORDAN *studies list.* JOE *and 7013 crane their*

11

necks, looking anxiously over his shoulder; finally.) Here we are: (*Reads.*) "Pendleton, Joseph—born 1914."

JOE. Right—April first. Huh! I get it now—*April first.*

JORDAN. (*Reading.*) "Mother's name, Mary; father's, Augustus."

JOE. Don't let *him* hear you call him Augustus.

JORDAN. "Both withdrawn and awaiting Joseph scheduled to join them . . . (*Snapping book closed; witheringly to* MESSENGER.) . . . the morning of May eleven, 1998!"

JOE. (*Excitedly.*) 1998! Why—why, that's *sixty years off yet!*

JORDAN. (*To the crestfallen* 7013; *dryly.*) It seems you were a bit premature.

JOE. (*Awed.*) *Sixty years more to go!* Gee! (*To* 7013.) You sure pulled a boner that time.

7013. (*Disgusted, to* JORDAN.) With all due respect to the Registrar, there must be a mistake—I—I may have been hasty, but certainly not by sixty years!

JORDAN. (*Snaps.*) The Registrar *never* makes mistakes.

7013. How any mortal could possibly have survived such a crash is beyond me.

JORDAN. (*Curtly.*) The point is, he *has!* How, is none of our concern.

7013. (*Meekly.*) Yes, sir. Of course, sir. I—I don't quite know what to say.

JORDAN. (*Peremptorily.*) Say nothing. *Take him back!*

7013. T-t-take him *back?*

JOE. Yeah, and the sooner the better. I got to get in trim for my "go" with the Alabama Bomber. If you fellas want to go see that scrap, I'll see if I can get you a couple of "comps." Come on—let's get going.

7013. But, Mr. Jordan, is it—is it possible to *return* Mr. Pendleton?

JORDAN. (*Irked.*) Certainly. Why not?

7013. (*Falteringly.*) But I—I rather thought this was the bourne from whence no traveler returneth!

JORDAN. (*Tartly.*) Mr. Pendleton didn't *travel* here. You *collected* him! We certainly can't have him hanging about for sixty years. Off with you.

7013. (*Feebly—at a terrible loss.*) Y-yes, sir. If you say so, sir. (*To* JOE.) Come along.

JOE. (*To* JORDAN.) Well, I'm sure glad I met you, Mr. Jordan. Thanks for straightening this thing out. Be seeing you in sixty years from now if you're still on the job. So long.

JORDAN. (*Smiles.*) Goodbye, Mr. Pendleton.

7013. (*To* JORDAN—*worriedly.*) I—I hope you won't report this, sir.

JORDAN. I'll have to ——

7013. (*Crushed.*) I beg of you—don't. It will wash me up. You see, the Chief wasn't too keen on putting me on. It was only through the most influential pressure and the outlook for a harvest even greater, alas, than 1914–1918, that he did so. (*Pleads.*) If you could overlook it this time, sir. It shan't happen again. I'll be scrupulously careful in the future. Really, I shall.

JORDAN. (*Kindly.*) Well, run along—I'll think about it.

7013. Yes, sir. Thank you, sir. (JOE *has moved up to one of the* PAS-SENGERS *who is about to enter the plane. As* 7013 *calls him.*) Come along, Mr. Pendleton.

JOE. (*To* PASSENGER.) H'ya, pal. This ain't such a bad place. I wouldn't mind stayin' only I got a lot of work to do yet. How about you? Did you finish your job?

(PASSENGER *smiles, nods, indicates "yes."*)

JOE. Okay then. Well—good luck!

(JOE, *now full of pep and hope, whistles as he quickly falls behind* 7013—*exit both* R.)

JORDAN. (*To* 2ND ESCORT.) Now, where were we?

2ND ESCORT. We had just checked in Mr. Kilija, sir.

JORDAN. (*Refers to his list.*) Oh, yes. All right. (*Warningly to* 2ND ESCORT.) Let 7013's error be a lesson to you. Don't be overly am-bitious. Exercise the degree of care and vigilance expected of you.

2ND ESCORT. Yes, sir. My record is one hundred percent.

JORDAN. See that you keep it so. Proceed.

2ND ESCORT. Porvoo, Anna.

JORDAN. (*Mumbles.*) Porvoo, Porvoo—check.

(MISS PORVOO *enters plane.*)

2ND ESCORT. Sillanpaa, Ralph.

JORDAN. Sillanpaa, Sillan—check.

(SILLANPAA *enters plane.*)

2ND ESCORT. That is all for this plane, sir. (*He salutes and exits* R.)

(7013 *and* JOE *re-enter, looking terribly worried.*)

JORDAN. (*Glares at them.*) Well, what now?

13

7013. (*Nervously.*) I—I'm frightfully sorry, sir, but—well—it—it's quite impossible to return to him.

JORDAN. (*Coming down to them—snaps.*) Impossible? Why?

7013. (*Distraught.*) I—I—you see, sir—oh, dear, this is *most* deplorable.

JOE. (*Mops his brow—frightened.*) Gosh! Gee!

JORDAN. (*Nettled—to 7013.*) I'm waiting.

JOE. (*Gulping.*) They done an awful thing to me, Mr. Jordan.

7013. By "they" he means his manager, Mr. Levene.

JOE. While you guys had me up here gabbing, the dumb cluck found my body in the plane and *had me cremated!*

7013. (*Miserably.*) I shall never forgive myself, sir.

JOE. (*Angrily.*) Wait till I get hold of Levene. I'll fix him. He can't go burning me up and get away with it!

JORDAN. (*Worriedly.*) That's bad, very bad. Complicates everything.

7013. I can't tell you how distressed I am. I feel *ghastly!*

JOE. How do you think *I* feel?

JORDAN. (*To 7013.*) I suppose I'll have to take charge of this. You finish checking in the rest of these passengers. (*Hands him list.*)

7013. Yes, sir.

JORDAN. (*To JOE.*) Come along, Joseph.

JOE. Where to?

JORDAN. I'm taking you back!

JOE. You can't. Didn't we just tell you? I ain't got a body any more?

JORDAN. What of it? I'll get you another body.

(JOE *and* 7013 *stare at* JORDAN *open-mouthed.*)

JOE. You'll do what?

7013. (*To JORDAN—amazed.*) Another body, sir?

JORDAN. (*Testily.*) That's what I said.

JOE. (*Hotly.*) Wait a minute, now—wait a minute. Not so fast. What kind of a deal is this?

JORDAN. Leave it to me, Joseph.

JOE. I'm leaving nothing to you. You guys ain't shovin' nobody's body on me! Not on your life!

7013. If Mr. Jordan says he'll get you another body, rest assured, Mr. Pendleton, it will be as good if not *better* than your own.

JOE. (*Belligerently.*) There ain't no better. I was built like a tank—I put in fifteen con-seck-ative years getting it "in the pink" an' I'm not losing it just because you guys fumbled the ball.

7013. But Joe, it's *gone! Your body doesn't exist any more!*

14

JOE. (*Doggedly.*) That ain't my fault. You fellas can do anything—now, come on—do your stuff!

JORDAN. (*Kindly.*) We shall, Joseph. You may have your choice of a thousand bodies. All excellent specimens.

7013. You hear that, Mr. Pendleton? Your choice of a thousand bodies. Think of it!

JOE. I am thinking of it, and I say no dice! I want my *own* body—nobody else's!

7013. Oh, tush! Don't make such a fuss! What is it, after all? A mere physical covering—worth, chemically—*just thirty-two* cents!

JOE. (*Hotly.*) Not *my* body—it was in the pink, I tell you!

7013. (*To* JORDAN, *who is studying the latest list.*) What have we available at the moment, sir? Something athletic? (*To* JOE.) You want to continue your pugilistic career, I suppose?

JOE. You suppose right. There ain't nothin' like it! (*Animatedly.*) The fame, the dough, the roar of the crowd, the lights, pictures in the paper ——

JORDAN. (*To* 7013.) I'm afraid we haven't much to offer him if that's the sort of thing he wants to do.

7013. (*To* JORDAN.) I've an idea, sir. Could we have him re-born?

JOE. (*Quickly.*) Nix—I'm not going through that again. Besides, what about my match with the Alabama Bomber? Re-born, huh? I couldn't make the weight in time.

JORDAN. Would you like to be rich, Joe—very rich?

JOE. Sure, and I'm gonna be. After I take the "Bomber" then I polish off "Killer" Gilbert, after which I put away that phony palooka, K. O. Murdock—then the million-dollar-gate and into my corner for the rest of my life sitting pretty—with maybe a restaurant or two just to keep me busy.

JORDAN. (*Smiling.*) You can have all that without fighting.

JOE. Naw, that wouldn't be any fun. I don't want anybody to hand me nothin'. I want to go out and get it myself.

7013. But, consider, Mr. Pendleton, you can have your choice—you can be anybody you like: a king, perhaps; or a prime minister; or a poet; or a ——

JOE. (*Interested for a moment.*) Gee—a guy like me—a swell king I'd make! (*Then shakes his head.*) No. Look, I'm just a mug! I wouldn't be good being anything else.

JORDAN. (*Smiling.*) We're all mugs, Joe.

7013. How about a dictator?

JOE. Who? Mussolini—or ——

15

7013. Someone similar; a very athletic fellow, powerfully built ——
JOE. What's his chest expansion? No. Forget it. I just want to be what I was—unless —— (*He looks sheepishly down at his saxophone.*) —is, uh—Rudy—no. Never mind.
JORDAN. Come along, Joe. (*He takes* JOE's *arm.*)
JOE. (*Holding back.*) Wait a minute. Let's get this thing straight before we go running around.
JORDAN. (*Smiling.*) I'll make it all clear to you as we go along. And don't worry, my boy. You'll be handsomely recompensed.
JOE. I only want what's coming to me—what I was an' what I was gonna be—nothin' more, nothin' less. It's up to you guys and *I expect you to make good!*
JORDAN. (*Smiling.*) We'll do our best, Joe. Come along.
JOE. (*Grudgingly.*) Okay—but I'm tipping you off—you're just wasting your time.
JORDAN. (*Smiling.*) We don't mind that here. (*He takes* JOE's *arm and they exit.*)
7013. Goodbye, Mr. Pendleton—the best of luck!

CURTAIN

ACT I

SCENE II: *The living-room in the Farnsworth Home.*

U.C. *are fairly large French doors, which remain open practically all the time. It is through these that* JORDAN *and* 7013 *make most of their entrances and exits. Another door, part way* D.R., *leads to the other rooms in the house, and another facing it* (L.) *leads to the outside and to kitchen and servants' quarters. The chief articles of furniture are a large and comfortable divan a little* L. *of* C. *and down stage; a radio a little to* R. *of* C. *entrance, a grand piano* U.L., *a desk* L. *of French doors, and various armchairs and smaller chairs as described. A medium-sized table just behind or at one side of divan. A few other objects, additional small tables or perhaps a small desk, can be used to dress the scene.*

An atmosphere of great wealth is present in every detail of the furnishings.

AT RISE: JORDAN and JOE, *who still carries his saxophone, enter* C. JORDAN *holds* JOE *by the hand, leading him as one would a bewildered child.* JOE *gapes in awe at the magnificence of the place.*

JOE. Pretty snazzy joint. (JORDAN, *weary, mops his brow with handkerchief and sinks exhausted into a chair.*) What's the matter, Mr. Jordan, tired?

JORDAN. No, Joe—merely weary.

JOE. That's because you're not in condition! You fellas ought to keep yourselves in better shape. Look at me—I ain't even puffin'.

JORDAN. It's not physical exhaustion that has me down. It's you— you're a job! I offer you the very cream of last week's crop and you turn a contemptuous nose at the lot.

JOE. There wasn't a physique in the bunch. I ain't letting you palm off no second-raters on me. You gotta keep in mind I was "in the pink."

JORDAN. That's becoming a most obnoxious color, Joe. Don't mention it again, please.

JOE. Okay.

JORDAN. (*Testily.*) Do you realize we've practically covered the universe? This is our hundred and thirtieth stop.

JOE. Yeah—we sure got around. Zip! We're in England! Zam! We're in Russia! Zowie! Australia! Wham! New York! How do you do it?

JORDAN. (*Smiles.*) That's a trade secret, Joe.

JOE. (*Looking around.*) I still can't get over the way we get in and out of places, right through locked doors, walking past people without being seen—why it—it's uncanny!

JORDAN. That's precisely the word.

JOE. I'd have sworn the maid saw us when we came in here—she looked straight at us. And those other gals brushing up against us— it's got me! Gee, you and Houdini woulda been a sensation in vaudeville! (JORDAN *laughs.*) Who's the guy you want me to size up here?

JORDAN. Jonathan Farnsworth.

JOE. Is he dead?

JORDAN. No.

JOE. Sick?

JORDAN. No.

JOE. Is he gonna meet with an accident?

JORDAN. No.

JOE. Then what are we doing here?

JORDAN. Don't ask so many questions.

JOE. I gotta ask questions. I want to know all about the body you want to hand me.

JORDAN. You'll be fully informed in good time.

JOE. What's he look like?

JORDAN. (*Wearily.*) Like twenty millions.

JOE. Yeah—but what shape is he in?

JORDAN. Joe, you must be prepared to sacrifice something for what you're getting. Surely, twenty millions is ample compensation for your body, no matter how pink it was.

JOE. The hell it is! There's nothin' better'n havin' the old chassis runnin' like a clock—in trim all the time—gettin' up in the mornin' feelin' like you could lick the heavyweight champ with one punch. Boy's that's terrific—that's havin' somethin' on the ball! (*Suddenly he hears somebody coming. He grabs* JORDAN *and fairly yanks him out of chair.*) Somebody's comin'. We better duck!

JORDAN. (*Shaking him off.*) Stop yanking me around. Can't you remember we can neither be seen nor heard?

JOE. (*Sheepishly.*) Oh, yeah, I keep forgetting. Excuse me. (*A* NURSE *enters* L., *carrying a glass of warm milk on a tray; over her arm is slung a red robe. Of course, she pays no attention to* JOE *or* JORDAN, *and as she nears them she speaks as it were through them to someone off-stage: "Thanks, Mrs. Ames, I have everything right here." She is a big, pleasant-looking Swede.* JOE *watches her as she crosses toward door down* R. *and exits.*) Is there a baby in the family?

JORDAN. No.

JOE. Then what's the nurse for?

JORDAN. She's attending Farnsworth.

JOE. But you said he wasn't sick.

JORDAN. He isn't, really; just a run-down condition.

JOE. (*Proudly.*) I ain't never had a run-down condition in my life. That's because ——

JORDAN. Yes, I know, Joe; you're "in the pink."

JOE. Right! (JORDAN *walks over to piano, sits down and starts playing.*) How long do we have to hang around here?

JORDAN. (*Playing.*) Until I collect Farnsworth.

JOE. You mean he's gotta go because of his run-down condition?

JORDAN. (*Calmly.*) No. He's being murdered!

JOE. Holy cow! (*Terrified, he stares at the imperturbable* JORDAN. *Excitedly.*) You mean it's goin' on right now? The murder.

18

JORDAN. Yes.

JOE. (*Eyes bulging.*) Here—in this house?

JORDAN. Yes.

JOE. (*Awed.*) Who—who's doing it?

JORDAN. Farnsworth's wife, and the man she's in love with!

JOE. Nice people you want me to meet. (JORDAN *laughs.*) How are they doing it?

JORDAN. (*Easily.*) They're drowning him in the bathtub.

JOE. (*Panicky.*) Jeez!! (*He again grabs* JORDAN's *arm.*) Come on, let's scram outa here before we get mixed up in it! (*He tries to pull* JORDAN *out* U.C. JORDAN *again shakes him off.*)

JORDAN. Wait!

JOE. Not me! I'll wait for you outside. I'm keepin' my nose clean. I'm in enough trouble already. (*He starts out.*)

JORDAN. Joe! (JOE *stops.*)

JOE. Look, Mr. Jordan, I'm not changing places with a guy who's got a wife like that hanging around. I'm not punch-drunk yet! (JORDAN *calmly continues playing piano*—JOE *stares at him.*) How can you sit there playing the piano while a guy's being knocked off?

JORDAN. This is my job, Joe.

JOE. You can have it! (*Looks fearfully at ceiling.*) This place gives me the creeps!

JORDAN. It's almost over, Joe.

JOE. Let's call the cops!

JORDAN. I'm afraid they'd pay no attention to us. (NURSE *re-enters* R., *without red robe and tray.* JOE *stares at her as she goes up-stage and exits* L. JORDAN *calmly.*) It's all over!

JOE. (*In a hushed voice.*) It—is? Gosh! Was the nurse in on it?

JORDAN. Innocently, yes.

JOE. How do you mean?

JORDAN. You'll soon find out.

(*As* JOE, *jittery, stares at ceiling,* TONY ABBOTT, *a handsome, suave, immaculate fellow of 35 enters* R., *calmly smoking cigarette.*)

JOE. (*Over to* JORDAN *at piano.*) Who's this?

JORDAN. Tony Abbott.

JOE. The mug the wife's in cahoots with?

JORDAN. (*Nods.*) Very much in cahoots.

JOE. Women sure are funny, falling for guys like him. What's he do?

JORDAN. He's Farnsworth's confidential secretary. He'll be **yours** when you're Farnsworth.

19

JOE. Like Hell he will, because I ain't gonna be Farnsworth!

(JULIA FARNSWORTH *enters,* R. *on this speech. She is a voluptuous, rather beautiful woman, about 30. She appears terribly nervous, in decided contrast to the calm* TONY.)

JORDAN. Mrs. Farnsworth, Joe.

JOE. (*Staring at her.*) Gee! She don't look like a killer.

JULIA. (*Jittery, as she crosses to* TONY.) Tony—I'm frightened.

TONY. (*Roughly.*) Steady.

JULIA. (*Finds it necessary to steady herself at table.*) I don't know what's suddenly come over me. I can't seem to shake off a feeling that there's something weird—something we can't see—hanging over us—watching us.

JOE. You said it, sister!

TONY. Perhaps a drink will steady you.

JULIA. (*Jittery.*) Yes.

JOE. I'm as nervous as she is!

(JULIA *goes to divan and sits while* TONY *crosses to table on which stand decanters of whiskey, a syphon of seltzer, ice cubes and glasses, and proceeds to fix drinks.*)

TONY. (*Reassuringly.*) We've nothing to fear. It will all come off just as we planned.

JOE. That's what *you* think!

TONY. What's more natural than after a glass of warm milk, a sleeping tablet or two, a tired, a *very* tired business man should—er—unfortunately—*drowse off* in his bath?

JOE. (*Hotly.*) Drowse off! Listen to the murdering bast —— (*Apologetically.*) Excuse me, Mr. Jordan.

JORDAN. (*Smiling.*) That's quite all right, Joe.

(TONY *now brings drinks over to* JULIA.)

TONY. (*Handing* JULIA *one, then holding his aloft.*) To twenty millions, my sweet!

JULIA. And us!

TONY. (*Smiles.*) Of course! (*They drink.*)

JOE. Come on, Mr. Jordan, get Farnsworth's soul and let's get the hell outa here!

JORDAN. Very well, Joe, but I did want you to meet a certain young lady who ——

JOE. Nix. I want nothin' to do with this bunch.

(MRS. AMES, *elderly, maternal type of housekeeper, enters* L.)

MRS. AMES. Miss Bette Logan is here to see Mr. Farnsworth.

(JULIA *becomes terribly nervous at mention of* BETTE, *but* TONY *flashes her a warning look.*)

TONY. (*To* MRS. AMES—*calmly.*) Show her in.

MRS. AMES. Yes, sir. (*She exits* L.)

TONY. (*Sharply.*) Julia—get hold of yourself!

JULIA. (*Steadying herself.*) I'll be all right, Tony.

TONY. You know what she's coming for. Be cordial, sympathetic. You can afford to be—*now!*

JULIA. Hold me close, Tony.

TONY. (*Embraces her—soothingly.*) Think only of what this means to us—happiness—freedom—no more of his vile tempers—no more of his ridicule. No more hiding. (*He kisses her.*)

JULIA. Whatever comes, darling, I shan't be sorry. I couldn't have gone on another day.

TONY. I'll be in the study. If she becomes difficult, bring her in to me. (*Kisses her again, pats her reassuringly, and quickly exits* R.)

JOE. Those two must be in love! (JORDAN *smiles.* JULIA *braces herself for the coming interview with* BETTE.) Is the dame who's coming in on the murder?

JORDAN. Judge for yourself.

(MRS. AMES *re-enters* L., *ushering in* BETTE LOGAN. *At sight of her* JOE *gasps in admiration—hopelessly fascinated—and with good reason, for* BETTE *is an unusually lovely young thing of about 20. At this moment, however, she appears cold, determined, grim.*)

MRS. AMES. (*Announcing.*) Here is Miss Logan, sir. (*Exits* L.)

JULIA. (*Now in complete control of herself—purrs.*) Good evening, Miss Logan.

BETTE. (*Coolly.*) Good evening, Mrs. Farnsworth.

(JOE *continues gaping admiringly at* BETTE—*spellbound. Puts saxophone down.*)

JOE. (*Almost reverently.*) Gee, Mr. Jordan, I didn't see anything in Heaven like that!

(JORDAN *smiles.*)

JULIA. Mr. Farnsworth is expecting you. He'll be right down, my dear.

JOE. What's she talking about? Farnsworth's dead, ain't he?
JORDAN. Quite!
JOE. Then how's he going to be right down?
JORDAN. Sh!

(JOE *subsides and returns his gaze to* BETTE.)

JULIA. Do sit down.
BETTE. Thank you. (*Sits.*)
JULIA. Drink?
BETTE. No—thank you.
JULIA. (*Tendering cigarette.*) Cigarette?
BETTE. Not just now.
JOE. That's right, kid, don't take anything from that dame.
JULIA. I just heard of your poor father's arrest. Too bad, but don't worry. I'm sure Mr. Farnsworth will help you. He seems particularly susceptible where you're concerned.
BETTE. I'm not here to ask for favors, Mrs. Farnsworth. My father is innocent.
JULIA. Of course. However, since he *is* the active head of Logan & Co., and since he *did* float the Bay Ridge securities ——
BETTE. (*Flashing.*) He was tricked by Farnsworth—but, of course, you and Mr. Abbott know that as well as I do.
JULIA. Aren't you a bit hysterical, my dear? Surely your father's not a child—he knew what he was doing.
BETTE. He was in Europe at the time. He left everything in Farnsworth's hands.
JULIA. Perhaps you'd better tell that to Mr. Abbott. He's in the study. I'm sure he can convince you that your father acted solely of his own accord. As a matter of fact, I happen to know it was strictly against the advice of my husband. But don't take my word for it. Come. (*She starts out* R. BETTE *stands a moment, undecided, then grimly strides out after* JULIA.)
JOE. (*Worriedly.*) Hey, I don't like to see that kid in there with those two killers.
JORDAN. She's perfectly safe.
JOE. Safe, my eye. She needs help. She's in trouble.
JORDAN. (*Gravely.*) Yes, Joe. Very serious trouble. She worships her father.
JOE. Well, you guys can do anything. Get busy. Help her!
JORDAN. *It's entirely up to Farnsworth!*

JOE. But he's dead!

JORDAN. Precisely! (JOE *stares uncomprehendingly at him.*) However, he wouldn't have helped her. The girl is right—Farnsworth engineered the entire affair—he tricked her father!

JOE. (*Angrily.*) And you want me to be Farnsworth and have a swell girl like that hate me!

JORDAN. Everyone builds himself, Joe, through the architectural power of the soul—the power to weave material into a fabric for its covering. You'll make a very different Farnsworth. *Spiritually,* there'll be no change in you!

JOE. Yeah, but she won't know that. She'll think I'm the same kind of a rat he is. No, sir, Mr. Jordan, I'd like to help her, but not this way.

JORDAN. (*Gently.*) There is no other way, Joe,

JOE. (*Miserably.*) Gee, you put me in a helluva tough spot.

JORDAN. On the contrary, you'll find it quite pleasant!

JOE. Yeah—how do you figure? I'd have to give up *everything:* my match with the Bomber, a chance at the title, my private life, everything. I wouldn't be myself any more and if a guy isn't himself, what good is he?

JORDAN. *You'll always be yourself, Joe!* Nothing can change that—you'll merely be using his physical covering—like donning a new overcoat!

JOE. It's got to be a pretty good overcoat to last me sixty years! (JORDAN *laughs. Weakening.*) Of course, I could build the guy up physically—like I did myself—couldn't I?

JORDAN. Of course.

JOE. Exercise, plain food, plenty of fresh air, regular hours, lots of ——

JORDAN. (*Smiling.*) I'm sure you'd do wonders with him. Your spirit will be young, vibrant, vital.

JOE. (*A thought strikes him.*) Hey—wait a minute! Will I fit him? I mean, will he fit me?

JORDAN. As you are now—purely spirit—I could put you inside a gnat!

JOE. (*Awed.*) A big guy like me?

JORDAN. Very comfortably.

JOE. Gee, you fellas can sure do tricks with us!

JORDAN. (*Smiling.*) To understand the physical body, you must first comprehend the nature of the earthly body. Discarding the atomic theory and eliminating ——

JOE. All I know about my body is that if I give it plenty of fresh air, plenty of exercise, plenty of wholesome food, plenty of ——
JORDAN. Yes, I know. It'll be "in the pink."
JOE. Can't miss!

(BETTE, JULIA *and* TONY *re-enter* R.)

TONY. (*To* BETTE.) Now that you've seen the correspondence between your father and Mr. Farnsworth, perhaps you realize ——
BETTE. There's nothing you can say or show me that will convince me that my father has done anything dishonest. He never took a penny from anyone. He couldn't. Now, will you tell Mr. Farnsworth I'm here, or must I go to his rooms unannounced?
JOE. (*Warningly to* BETTE.) Don't do it, Miss Logan, or you'll get yourself mixed up in the killing.
TONY. (*Smiling.*) I'll have you announced at once, Miss Logan. (*He walks upstage and pulls bell-cord* L. *of* C. *entrance.*)
JULIA. Whether your father is guilty or not isn't important, really. What *is* important is that you're here to—shall we politely say—*intercede* for him.
BETTE. I'll do anything to save my father.
JULIA. Yes, I know—*anything!*

(MRS. AMES *enters* L.)

MRS. AMES. You rang, Madam?
JULIA. Yes. *Tell Mr. Farnsworth Miss Logan is here.*
MRS. AMES. Very well, Madam. (*Exits* R.)
JOE. What's the idea? That dame knows Farnsworth is dead!
JORDAN. You haven't much time to decide, Joe.
JOE. (*Worriedly.*) You mean whether I want to be Farnsworth?
JORDAN. I mean whether you want to help that girl.
JOE. Gee, sure I do, only, only ——
JORDAN. Hurry, Joe.
JOE. Don't rush me. This is a pretty important step in my life, you know. (JORDAN *nods.* JOE *continues—gulping.*) Look—if I do it, it'll only be temporary, won't it?
JORDAN. If you wish it.
JOE. (*Emphatically.*) You bet I do. Just until I get her straightened out. Better get that clear.
JORDAN. (*Smiling.*) It's quite clear, my boy.
JOE. Okay—*it's a deal!*

JORDAN. Come! (*He holds out his hand*—JOE *timidly takes it, and the two start out* C. *As* JOE *passes* BETTE.)

JOE. (*Gently.*) Don't worry, Bette—I mean, Miss Logan. I'm moving into Farnsworth—everything's gonna be all right—— (*He looks at* JORDAN.)—I hope! (*As he nears* C. *door with* JORDAN—*frightened.*) Gosh, Mr. Jordan, I'm beginning to feel funny already!

JULIA. (*To* BETTE.) I heard my beloved reserved a stateroom on the Ile de France, sailing Wednesday. Of course you'll sail with him—for your father's sake, naturally! (BETTE *stares contemptuously at* JULIA.) Paris! Enchanting this time of year. The flowers in the Bois! Pretty, new clothes; music; dancing; divine, really. You must let me give you a list. There are so many charming places where he and I spent our honeymoon, I shouldn't want you to miss them!

BETTE. I see where I have overestimated you, Mrs. Farnsworth, I hardly thought you'd permit such an arrangement.

JULIA. (*Shrugging her shoulders.*) Why not? It wouldn't last. It never has. I know my husband. He's a fool for a pretty face. You'd merely be another feather in his cap!

BETTE. As you are!

TONY. (*Laughing.*) Your round, Miss Logan.

(*As* JULIA *seethes,* MRS. AMES *re-enters* R. *All look at her—*JULIA *and* TONY *are terribly nervous, waiting for the dread announcement.*)

MRS. AMES. (*To* BETTE.) *Mr. Farnsworth will be right down, Miss Logan!*

(*It's a bombshell to* JULIA *and* TONY, *who can only gape foolishly, unbelievingly at* MRS. AMES, *as curtain falls.*)

CURTAIN

ACT II

Same.—Part of the living-room is now converted into a gymnasium; pulleys, weights, bag-punching platform, etc., have been installed.

TIME: *The next morning.*

NOTE: *A few moments before rise of curtain we hear some very expert and rhythmic bag-punching.*

AT RISE: JOE, *now resplendent in the same red robe used in previous scene—monogrammed* "J. F."—*is energetically punching bag while* JORDAN *watches, amused, one leg comfortably thrown over the other as he sits on divan.*

JOE'S *physical appearance is in no way altered when he becomes Farnsworth. Since, spiritually, he never changes, it is important that the audience continues seeing him as* JOE *throughout the play; it is* ONLY THE CHARACTERS—*with the exception of* JORDAN *and* 7013—*who see him as Farnsworth, and later as K. O. Murdock. In this way, the audience is given the omniscience of Heaven and see* JOE *as he actually is.*

JOE. (*Punching away; then stops.*) Say, this ain't so bad. Mr. Farnsworth fits me like a glove. A bit flabby here and there, but I'll soon fix that.

JORDAN. I told you you'd be perfectly comfortable.

JOE. Yeah—but I can't get it through my head that I'm him now.

JORDAN. (*Smiling.*) You'll get accustomed to it.

JOE. I really look like him?

JORDAN. Of course

JOE. Maybe it's this red robe of his —— (*He throws it off and stands attired in a pair of purple gym ,runks.*) Now?

JORDAN. You're *Farnsworth,* Joe.

JOE. I suppose if a guy like you says so, it's so; only what gets me is I still *feel* the same, and I *talk* the same. I don't feel any change.

JORDAN. (*Smiling.*) Don't vex your mind about it, Joe. It is at once too simple and too complex for your easy comprehension. *Inwardly,* you haven't changed—you're still Joe Pendleton; *outwardly* you're Jonathan Farnsworth, believe me.

JOE. Oh, I believe you all right, but what about Mrs. Farnsworth? I won't be able to fool her.

JORDAN. (*Smiling.*) You already have. Very successfully, too.

JOE. (*Slowly.*) Yeah, yeah, I sure did. (*Grins.*) When she saw me come down out of that bathroom she looked like she saw a ghost!

JORDAN. (*Smiles.*) It amounted to that.

JOE. Is the doctor still with her?

JORDAN. Yes, but she'll be all right. She's gradually getting over the shock.

JOE. How's Tony—my confidential secretary? He looked pretty pale around the gills, too, when I came in and said, "Hello, Miss Logan, glad to see you!" (JORDAN *laughs.* JOE *continues proudly.*) I did that pretty good, don't you think?

JORDAN. (*Smiling.*) You were superb!

JOE. I musta been. Why, even Bette thought I was Farnsworth.

JORDAN. Of course.

JOE. I told her to see me this morning and I'd get her father all fixed up. But how am I going to do it?

JORDAN. You'll find it a comparatively simple task.

JOE. I don't know about that. I'm not very smart, you know. How am I going to be able to catch on to all this *fin*ance stuff—the stocks and bonds and *deb*-entures?

JORDAN. De*ben*tures, Joe!

JOE. Yeah—Farnsworth's desk is full of that crap.

JORDAN. (*Smiling.*) *Your* desk. You'll be surprised how easily it will all come to you.

JOE. Well, you stick close to me till I get the hang of things.

JORDAN. I'll be glad to.

JOE. (*Grinning.*) Can you imagine how the Police Department will feel if this ever comes out? Here's a big financier drowned in his bathtub by his wife and her honey, and then comes back to life again and the cops don't even know the guy was sick. (JORDAN *smiles.*) It's got me. How do you fellas do it?

JORDAN. (*Smiling.*) If there were no mystery left to explore, Joe, one would lose the spiritual joy of contemplating the workings of the Universe. Life would be rather dull.

JOE. You guys have an alibi for everything. (*A sudden, distant, muted note like the wail of a horn; it is eerie in effect, yet not unpleasant. Freezing.*) Did you hear that?

JORDAN. (*Rises.*) I must go, Joe.

JOE. They're paging you, eh?

JORDAN. I'll be back. (*And he is gone,* C.)

(JOE's *reverie is interrupted by entrance of a* WORKMAN *in overalls carrying a rowing machine, accompanied by* ANN, *another housemaid. She gives him a hand. They enter* L.)

WORKMAN. (*To* JOE.) Where'll I put this, Mr. Farnsworth?

JOE. You mean me?

WORKMAN. Sure—Mr. Farnsworth!

JOE. (*Gulping.*) Yeah—I heard you. Just set it down over there.

(WORKMAN *carries machine over.*)

WORKMAN. I was watching you at that bag before, Mr. Farnsworth. You sure can make it dance.

JOE. Aw, that wasn't anything, these joints are a little tight yet —— (*As he stretches and limbers.*) —but wait till I'm back in form. I'll make this pigskin yodel.

ANN. You cert'nly keep yourself in trim, sir.

JOE. I gotta. The Bomber's no setup, you know, and I only got a short time to get myself in shape.

WORKMAN. (*Smiles; thinks he's being spoofed.*) You look pretty good right now, Mr. Farnsworth.

JOE. Not good enough for the Bomber. He's tough.

ANN. (*Gaping at* JOE.) You mean you're planning to fight the Bomber, sir?

JOE. (*To* ANN.) You're bright, you are. I've been getting ready for him for six months—an' let me tip you off to something—I'll lick the be-jeez out of him. Then I'll do likewise to Murdock.

WORKMAN. You've got a reputation as a sportsman, and you're a swell polo player—but, I didn't know you went in for professional boxing. I thought you were just a banker.

JOE. Naw, that's something I just took up lately.

WORKMAN. Kiddin' us now, ain't you, Mr. Farnsworth? I've been seeing your picture on the financial page for years.

JOE. You mean *sporting page.* (WORKMAN *and* ANN *stare at him.*) Look, fellas, tell me straight—this picture you see of me in the—the financial page—does it look like me?

ANN. Spittin' image of you—Er—sir.

(*As* JOE *stares at* WORKMAN *and* ANN, *they exit* L. JOE *scratches head, then goes to rowing machine and tries it.*)

(TONY *enters* R. *and stands gaping at* JOE, *rowing machine and other apparatus.*)

TONY. (*Trying to be pleasant.*) Good morning, Mr. F. Well, you certainly look like a new man today.

JOE. Yeah? How do you mean—*new?*

TONY. You're looking very fit.

JOE. I do, eh?

TONY. Remarkably so. (*He turns to desk.*)

JOE. (*Rowing.*) Where's that old dame that lets people in and out of this joint?

TONY. (*Stares at* JOE.) I'm afraid I don't understand you.

JOE. (*Stops rowing.*) Oh, you don't? Well, get this: you and me are going to tangle plenty unless you watch your step. I'm on to you, so don't try any funny business—*and stay out of my bathroom*—understand?

TONY. (*Gaping at him.*) Really, Mr. F.!

JOE. Cut that "Mr. F." stuff, and go get that old dame in here.

TONY. (*Shrugs his shoulders.*) Of course, you mean Mrs. Ames? (*He pulls bellcord; then coming down to* JOE.) I'm beginning to be alarmed about you.

JOE. Yeah—why?

TONY. (*With a sweep of his hand at apparatus.*) This. It's much too strenuous for your blood pressure.

JOE. My blood pressure is perfect—always was. Why, I used to give transfusions at the hospital once a week—the docs there told me they never seen such blood.

TONY. (*Staring at* JOE, *certain he's out of his mind.*) Indeed! I wasn't aware of the fact.

JOE. There's a lot around here you ain't in on.

(MRS. AMES *enters* L.)

MRS. AMES. (*Exchanges glances with* TONY, *then crosses to* JOE, *now rowing vigorously.*) You rang, sir?

JOE. Huh? Oh, yeah. (*Stops rowing.*) Now, get this, Mrs. Whoozis —and get it straight! When Miss Logan calls, you let me know right away. Understand?

MRS. AMES. Yes, sir. (*Coughs worriedly.*) Er—what attire shall you be wanting this morning, sir? Mansfield wishes to know.

TONY. Top hat and morning suit, Mrs. Ames.

JOE. Hey—wait a minute. What kind of an outfit is that?

TONY. You're opening the new bridge today, sir. You and the Mayor are cutting the ribbon. (*Laughs in an attempt to be jolly.*)

JOE. I'm cutting a ribbon? What the hell *is* this?

TONY. There's no getting out of it, sir. The Mayor insisted.

MRS. AMES. A messenger has just brought your steamship tickets, sir.

(TONY *takes them from* MRS. AMES.)

JOE. What steamship tickets?

TONY. The Ile de France. You're sailing Wednesday.

JOE. I am? Where am I going?

(MRS. AMES, *with a frightened glance, exits* R.)

TONY. You—you didn't choose to tell me, sir. You merely told me to get two tickets.

JOE. Two? Who's going with me?

TONY. (*With a smile.*) I really haven't the least idea, Mr. F.

JOE. Well, I ain't going. I got work to do right here. Cancel them. And this ribbon-cutting business is out, too. Ribbon! What do they think I am! (*Starts to row again.* TONY *gapes at him. After a moment, stops rowing.*) That reminds me—I gotta write a letter.

TONY. Yes, sir. (*Coming forward with pencil and book.*)

JOE. (*Sees* TONY's *pencil poised for duty.*) Oh—okay. This letter is going to Jim Rafferty, Manager, McGovern, Rafferty & Blunt, Jersey City. Um—let me see —— (*Begins to pace like a businessman he once saw in the throes of dictation.*) Start off like this: "Dear Boss: I want to apologize for smashing up the Company's plans but it wasn't my fault exactly. You see, it was like this. I—I—uh ——" (*He scratches his head as* TONY *stares at him, not writing down a word* JOE *says.* JOE *is too absorbed trying to frame the letter to notice this.*) "I—was just passing over Toledo, playing some hot licks on my sax, when—when—uh—all of a sudden some gimmick goes haywire and—uh—before I knew it, the ship is heading for a crash. Some mug I couldn't see hops on the plane—out of nowhere—uh ——" (*Scratches his head.*) "—the guy is a messenger from heav ——" (*It is all becoming a little difficult. To* TONY.) Wait a minute. Cut that last part. Say: "I was headin' for a terrible crash. Down I was going like a bat out of hell, and just before I was killed, I was saved ——" No—no—geez, they'll think I've gone screwy. "Just before I was killed, this guy who hopped on, grabs my soul—" (*To* TONY.) To hell with it. Just say: "I can't explain it exactly and you wouldn't believe me, anyway, but I just want you to know I'll pay for the

30

damage I done." Sign it: "Yours truly, Joe." Oh—and put a P. S. on it: "P. S.: I saved the sax!" (*Finishes dictating and looks at the astounded* TONY.) Did you get that down?

TONY. Are you sure you're—er—quite well?

JOE. If you think there's anything the matter with me, just put these on. (*He tosses a pair of boxing gloves to* TONY, *who catches them, but immediately puts them down.*)

TONY. Really, Mr. Farnsworth, don't you think we'd better get to the business at hand? There's the very devil stirring this morning. The Equitable crowd demand a showdown—they want to know why you sold A & O 1942 3½'s and reversed your position on Air Carbide. Also, we've got to do something about the P. & R. Debentures.

JOE. (*With a knowing nod, rather enjoying all this.*) Oh yes, the Debentures. Yes, I've been—uh—talking about those —— (*Being near at the moment to the door* c., *through which* JORDAN *left, he looks heavenward.*) —with a pal of mine!

TONY. (*Busy with papers.*) You mean J. P., of course? (*Comes forward with papers.*)

JOE. No—just J. His name is Jordan.

TONY. Jordan?

JOE. Yeah. I'd like you to meet him—soon!

TONY. I should like to, very much. (*Indicating slip of paper.*) Here's a memo from Gibbons. He thinks we should go "long" ten million bushels July wheat.

JOE. He does, eh?

TONY. Yes—immediately.

JOE. Ten million bushels of wheat, eh? Where'll we put it? (*Sits with feet on table, in what he believes is a big businessman's posture.*) How about twenty million boxes cornflakes?

TONY. Have your little joke, sir, but seriously—we need it, to hedge our June position.

JOE. Oh we do, eh? Well, well, well! Ten million bushels of wheat? Tell you what you do. Order a million gallons of sweet cream. As long as we have the wheat, we might as well eat it. What else is on your mind?

TONY. (*Looks at him; then.*) There are a hundred things demanding your attention this morning—the Tracy Collateral Trust, the Homestate Stock option warrants, the Southern Central Merger, the Rawlins Amortization ——

JOE. Hey, look—I'm too busy to go into all that today.

TONY. But, surely, Mr. F., you can't possibly ignore —— ?

31

JOE. I ain't interested in anything today except getting that girl Bette —I mean, Miss Logan—straightened out. Now, what's all this business about putting her father in jail?

TONY. Inasmuch as you engineered the entire affair ——

JOE. (*Angrily.*) Listen, you—I had nothing to do with it, see? And I don't care what he done—any guy who's got a daughter like Bette, must be an all right guy and you lay off him—get me?

(JOE *crosses over as if he might sock* TONY, *but* JULIA's *entrance* R. *interrupts him.*)

JULIA. (*To* JOE.) Jonathan!

JOE. (*Hurriedly dons his robe; embarrassed.*) Ex—excuse me. Feeling better after your faint?

JULIA. (*Crossing to* JOE.) I'm all right, dear—just a dizzy spell. (*He keeps backing away from her.*) But, darling, I'm worried about *you!* What is the meaning of all this? (*Indicates the changed room.*)

JOE. (*Maneuvering himself so divan is between them.*) I gotta have a gym. I gotta keep in trim.

JULIA. But this is the living-room.

JOE. I don't need a living-room. I can live in any room, but I need a gym and this is the biggest room in the house, so I took it.

JULIA. You—you don't seem to be the same person this morning.

JOE. No? Who do you think I am? Take a good look.

JULIA. Darling, you frighten me.

JOE. You scare me, too.

JULIA. You know how very much I worry about you. (*Starting to move around to him.*)

JOE. (*Grimly, edging further away.*) Yeah—I'll bet you do.

JULIA. You must be very careful not to strain yourself. Remember what the doctor told you about over-exertion. Your blood-pressure, your heart ——

JOE. I'll have this body "in the pink" in a week. (*Turning away.*)

JULIA. Do be careful, dearest. I couldn't bear it if anything happened to you. (*Crossing to him, attempts to caress him.*)

JOE. (*Undraping her arms from his neck.*) Look—I—I've been having a pretty good workout—and I gotta take a bath! (*He starts out* R., *door, meaningly.*) *And I don't need any help from you two, get me?* (*Exits* R. *as* JULIA *and* TONY *gape after him.*)

JULIA. What do you make of it? This incredible change in him?

TONY. The water must have affected his brain.

JULIA. It's not Jonathan—it *can't* be!

TONY. If we hadn't seen him come down out of the bathroom grinning like a hyena, I'd be inclined to agree with you, my dear.

JULIA. (*Shudders.*) It—it's creepy. I get a cold chill looking at him.

TONY. I don't feel any too comfortable myself. I was certain he was *dead!* We held him under long enough.

JULIA. What do you suppose this sudden mania for all this —— (*She indicates apparatus.*) can be? (TONY *shrugs.*) He's playing a game with us. Oh, Tony, I—I'm afraid. (*She takes hold of him—he embraces her.*) We must do something. I couldn't spend another night in this house!

TONY. (*Grimly.*) There'll be no bungling this time. (*He crosses to desk and takes gun, which he pockets.*)

(MRS. AMES *enters* L.)

MRS. AMES. (*Announcing.*) A Mr. Max Levene is here to see Mr. Farnsworth.

TONY. (*To* JULIA.) He doesn't know any Levene.

MRS. AMES. Shall I send him away, sir?

TONY. No. Show him in.

MRS. AMES. Yes, sir. (*Exits* L.)

JULIA. (*Warningly.*) Be on your guard, darling, he may be one of Jonathan's investigators.

TONY. We'll soon find out. (TONY *looks to make sure gun is loaded, returns it to hip pocket.*)

(MRS. AMES *re-enters* L. *and announces.*)

MRS. AMES. Mr. Max Levene.

(MAX LEVENE *enters* L., *a shrewd, pugnacious, typical fight manager.* MRS. AMES *exits* L.)

MAX. (*To* TONY, *questioningly.*) Mr. Farnsworth?

TONY. I'm Mr. Abbott.

MAX. Glad to meet you, Mr. Abbott.

TONY. I'm Jonathan Farnsworth's confidential man.

MAX. Then maybe you can tell me what he wants with me?

TONY. Probably—that is, if you'd be good enough to tell me what sort of business you're in, Mr. Levene.

MAX. Me? I'm in the fight racket. I'm a manager. I manage fighters.

JULIA. I can't possibly imagine what my husband would want with a—a fight manager.

TONY. Nor I.

(*As* JULIA *and* TONY *stare puzzled at him* MAX *takes in gymnastic appurtenances.*)

MAX. I see he goes in for athletics. Maybe he's thinking of entering the ring. You know—the squared circle.

TONY. Don't be absurd, my man. If you'll state your business, I'll write you a letter ——

MAX. Say, don't go to getting snooty with me. I got a telegram from Farnsworth to be here and ——

(*He stops as* JOE *enters* R. *He is now fully dressed in morning suit. He sees* MAX *and grinning broadly, quickly strides over to him.*)

JOE. (*Cordially slapping the bewildered* MAX *on the back.*) Max— you old son-of-a-gun. How are you? (TONY, JULIA *and* MAX *gape astonished at* JOE.) Jeez, I'm glad to see you!

MAX. You know me?

JOE. (*Laughs.*) Know you? I ought to know you, you dirty, double-crossing ba—— (*Realizing* JULIA *is present, he stops.*) How do you like my monkey suit? This is morning clothes, mug; I got special suits for morning, afternoons, evenings—I'm a regular primer-donna.

(MRS. AMES *has entered* L., *bringing top hat which she offers to* JOE.)

MRS. AMES. Your hat, sir.

JOE. Listen, you, I only put this on for laughs—I knew *he* was coming. (*To* TONY *and* JULIA.) You two scram—I—I got some private business with my pal, Max.

JULIA. (*Flushing.*) How dare you talk like that to me?

TONY. Come, Mrs. Farnsworth.

JULIA. (*To* JOE.) I can't imagine what's come over you, darling.

JOE. I'm okay. And the less you worry about me, the better I like it. Now—beat it!

JULIA. (*Controlling her anger.*) I'm going to call Dr. Evans, and ——

JOE. Don't go calling nobody; just leave me alone. (JULIA *would say more but* TONY *motions silence. Together they go off;* MRS. AMES *glad to join them. The* THREE *exit* R.) That dame gets my goat! (*To* MAX.) Take a good look at me, Max—don't you know me?

MAX. Sure—sure, I know you; everybody knows you, Mr. Farnsworth.

JOE. Where are your eyes, you dumb ox? I'm not Farnsworth—I'm Joe Pendleton—your Joe.

34

MAX. You're nuts, Mr. Farnsworth.

JOE. Look, Max. Maybe I don't look like Joe any more, but I swear I'm him, just the same. And it's all *your* fault.

MAX. My fault?

JOE. Yeah. If you wasn't in such a goddam hurry to cremate my body, I wouldn't be in this jam now.

MAX. (*Patiently.*) Take it easy, Mr. Farnsworth. Your wife was right. You need a doctor.

JOE. You'll need one soon unless ———

MAX. Look, I'm a busy man. If you're screwy ———

(JORDAN *suddenly appears at door* C. *and saunters in smiling—*JOE *seeing him.*)

JOE. (*To* JORDAN.) You're just the guy I want. I want you to prove something. (MAX *of course, unable to see or hear* JORDAN, *becomes even more uncomfortable. He is sure* JOE *is completely nuts.* JOE *continues.*) Tell him what happened, Mr. Jordan. Oh, this is Max Levene, my manager. He's the guy cremated me. Max, this is Mr. Jordan.

MAX. (*Humoring him.*) Glad to meet you, Mr. Jordan. (*Shakes hands with himself, mops his brow.*) Say, how about a little drink? The *three* of us? (*Going up to decanter on table.*)

JOE. Sure, help yourself; I forgot, Max, you can't see him.

MAX. Maybe I will after I have a couple.

JOE. You can't see him because you ain't dead yet.

MAX. I ain't nuts, either. (*He has filled three glasses and now places them on table.*) Well, I got mine—and here's yours—and if the other one disappears, I'm taking a taxi to the booby-hatch. (*He glues his eyes on third glass and waits.*)

(JORDAN *stands up strange, silent and amused.*)

(MESSENGER 7013 *steps in at door* C.)

JOE. Excuse me, Max. The guy who fumbled the whole thing just came in.

(MAX *looks up, sees no one, takes quick look around room and as* JOE *crosses toward him.*)

MAX. Sure—I see him, Mr. Farnsworth. He's got on a high hat and spats. (*He quickly swallows other two drinks, then*) Now, I know all you fellows have a lot of business to talk over, so I'll be mooching along ———

JOE. (*Stopping him.*) No, you don't. You're staying here till we talk this over. (*He drops* MAX *into seat.* MAX *is now watching for a chance to get out as he listens to* JOE *carrying on a conversation with "himself." To* 7013.) Well, what's the dope?

7013. (*To* JORDAN.) Haven't you told him yet, sir?

JORDAN. No.

7013. The Chief knows the situation and is storming all over the place —— (*Wryly.*) You know how effectually he can storm.

JORDAN. (*Impatiently.*) Yes, yes, go on.

7013. It seems the thing is far more serious than we thought: Mr. Pendleton was meant to be the world's next pugilistic champion, and ——

JOE. (*Jubilantly.*) I knew it. I knew nobody could stop me. (*To* MAX, *excitedly.*) Didja hear that, Max? I'm gonna be champ! (MAX *nods* "sure.") You'll make a pile of tin with me —— (*Angrily.*) —and you go burning my body! I ought to slug you. (MAX *cowers and rises in an attempt to leave* L., *but* JOE *grabs him and pulls him savagely back. To* 7013.) Go ahead—tell me more.

7013. There's nothing more to tell you, Mr. Pendleton. I've been everywhere searching for a specimen whose physical and fistic qualifications measure up; I'm in the dog-house until I've made good my blunder.

JOE. Well, you better shake a leg. I don't want to use this body any longer that I have to.

7013. There's a strapping fellow—in Australia—a wrestler—wild sort—he'll soon be available—drunk driving ——

JOE. Who is he? I'll tip him to lay off the liquor.

7013. Don't you want him?

JOE. What's his weight?

7013. 198 pounds.

JOE. Too heavy. What's his reach?

7013. Seventy-eight inches.

JOE. (*To* MAX, *who is gaping at* JOE.) What do you think, Max?

MAX. I think I ought to get the hell out of here. (*He starts out* L., *but again* JOE *pulls him back.*)

JOE. What's the matter with you? You want to run out on a million dollars? Sit down! (*He literally flings* MAX *into a chair, then turns to* 7013.) Look—get me all the dope on this "Aussie"; chest expansion, biceps, forearm—everything—and see what else you can dig up.

7013. Yes, Mr. Pendleton. (*He has crossed to door* C.) Gentlemen! (*With a salute, he is gone* C.)

36

JOE. (*To* JORDAN, *worriedly.*) Look, Mr. Jordan, I gotta get all this over to Max here; I gotta make him believe what's happened; that I'm Joe Pendleton. He's a swell manager and I need him. I'd feel lost in the ring without him. Can't you let him see you? Just until I can make him understand?

JORDAN. You can do it yourself, Joe. Try.

JOE. I can? (JORDAN *nods.* JOE *looks dubiously at* JORDAN *a moment, then turns to* MAX, *who has been sitting there gaping at him. To* MAX, *earnestly.*) Look, Max, you gotta believe I'm your Joe. Listen—remember those airplane trips I used to make three times a week between Jersey and Omaha? Well, the last trip something went flooey and the ship started to fall. This guy who was just here, who you couldn't see on account you're not dead yet, saw me fall. Oh, I forgot to tell you, he's a messenger—they got a whole army of guys like him who go around collecting people. You see, with all the wars going on and everything, it's a pretty busy season. Well, this guy pulled a boner and took me before I was dead—and now, he's got to make good—get it?

MAX. Sure, I get it. Now, I'll tell you what you ought to get—a doctor —the best there is!

JOE. (*Angrily.*) I'm gonna make you believe me if I have to pound you to a jelly. How would I know all about this Joe if I wasn't Joe? Look—you've got forty percent of me ——

MAX. I have? Well, that's pretty nice, but since when did you give me a piece of you?

JOE. Since that time in Astoria when you saw me put away "Butcher Boy" McKenzie. (MAX *stares harder at* JOE.) You told me I had "color"; I was what the fans wanted—like the Manassa Mauler! Remember? (MAX's *eyes grow larger as he stares at* JOE.) And you got a sister named Rosie who ain't married yet, but she's got three kids, and ——

MAX. Pipe down on that! Somebody might hear. How do you know about my family?

JOE. 'Cause I'm Joe, you dope. An' I can tell you a lot more—like, for instance, that night on the boat to Albany when your wife, Lena, caught you.

MAX. Say—who in the hell are you, anyway?

JOE. (*Heatedly.*) I'm trying to tell you. I'm Joe—your Joe—I'm in Farnsworth's body because I couldn't get back into mine on account of you being in such a hurry to burn it, you big stiff! Watch, I'll prove it to you. (*He hurries over to a corner of the room and brings*

his saxophone out from near desk, brings it to MAX.) Remember this?
MAX. (*Examines it, his eyes go wider and he dabs a tear away.*) Sure
—that's Joe's—poor Joe!
JOE. Cut the phony tears—this ought to prove I'm telling you the truth.
MAX. Where did you get it?
JOE. (*Shouts.*) It's mine, I tell you. Listen—I'll play you something you always liked to hear me play. (*He plays a part of a tune, none too well;* MAX *is chilled to the bone as he recognizes it.*)
MAX. (*Hushed.*) It's just like coming from the dead.
JOE. Now—do you believe me? You think Farnsworth could play like that? And here's something more. Remember our old grip? (*He extends hand—*MAX *takes it—and they go through some secret manipulating which now definitely convinces* MAX.)
MAX. (*Shouts.*) JOE—Oh, my Lord! *JOE!!*

(MAX *promptly starts to fall as though in a faint.*)

(JOE *catches him and looks at* JORDAN.)

JOE. (*Joyfully.*) He knows me—he knows me! (*He frantically starts fanning* MAX, *brings him over to a chair and starts massaging his wrists.*) Max—Max—speak to me —— (*After a moment* MAX *"comes to" and stares at* JOE.)
MAX. (*Faintly.*) I'm seeing things—no, I'm not—it must be the hang-over from last night.
JOE. No, it ain't, Max—It's me all right—your Joe!
MAX. You're really Joe?
JOE. Just inside. Outside, I'm Farnsworth the banker!
MAX. How'd you get into Farnsworth?
JOE. They put me in it after he was drowned —— (MAX *blinks at* JOE.) —but it's just temporary—just till I get a swell girl out of a jam—oh, boy, and has she got plenty of zing!! (*To* JORDAN.) Is that right, Mr. Jordan?
JORDAN. Yes, Joe.
MAX. Say, maybe *I'm* somebody else, too. I wonder whose body *I'M* in? (*After a futile look all about him.*) Ask your friend. (*Hastily.*) No, better not. If I'm somebody else, I don't want to know about it.
JOE. Now, look, Max. If I'm going to be champ, I got to keep in trim. I don't want to lose my punch. You got to get busy and get me some fights right away. First, the Bomber—then "K. O." Murdock, that palooka, then ——

38

MAX. Wait a minute. Maybe *I* think you're Joe Pendleton—I said *maybe*—but it's going to be awful hard to get it over with the Boxing Commission. The regulations bar ghosts.

JOE. I'm no ghost. I'm not dead. I got sixty years to go yet! (*Gets an idea—excitedly to* MAX.) Look—who's the logical contender for a match with the "Bomber"?

MAX. You was ——

JOE. I know I was—but who is now?

MAX. "Killer" Gilbert.

JOE. Match me with him.

MAX. You're crazy. "Killer" won't meet Farnsworth the banker.

JOE. Offer him dough. Fix it. You can do it.

MAX. Where am I going to get dough?

JOE. (*To* JORDAN.) Where is he going to get dough?

JORDAN. From you. Write him a check.

JOE. I ain't got a button.

JORDAN. You keep forgetting you're Farnsworth. Call your secretary. He'll make it out for you.

JOE. He will?

JORDAN. Of course.

JOE. You're sure it'll be all right?

JORDAN. It'll be quite all right.

JOE. Okay—if you say so. (*He goes over and pulls bell-cord. To* MAX.) How much will you need to fix the match?

MAX. Twenty grand.

JOE. That's a lot of dough.

MAX. It's worth it to fix a fight for a ghost.

(MRS. AMES *enters* L.)

MRS. AMES. (*To* JOE.) You rang, sir?

JOE. Yeah. Send my *seck*-atary in.

MRS. AMES. Your secretary? I'll ask him to come right in. (*As she starts exiting* R.)

JOE. Wait —— (MRS. AMES *stops, and looks inquiringly at* JOE.) Has Miss Logan been around?

MRS. AMES. Not yet, sir.

JOE. Well, bring her in as soon as she shows up.

MRS. AMES. Of course, sir. (*Exits* R.)

MAX. (*Staring at* JOE, *still unable to grasp it.*) I can't get over you, Joe; a mug like you turned into a big shot like Farnsworth. Hey, maybe your invisible pal here can make me Rockefeller!

39

JOE. Naw—stay the way you are, Max. Take my advice.

MAX. Look, Joe, what do you want to fight any more for? With all Farnsworth's dough, you got the world right in your back pocket. Why, he owns five or six banks—you can walk into any one of them and clean out the ——

JOE. What do you take me for? I don't want any of his dough—and I don't want to be him any longer than I have to. I'll have all the dough I need when I'm champ. (*Animatedly.*) Oh, boy, I can hardly wait to climb in the ropes again—the roar of the crowd, the lights, the battle for ——

(TONY *enters* R.)

TONY. Yes, Mr. F.?

JOE. (*To* JORDAN *apprehensively.*) You're sure it's okay?

(TONY *looks to see who* JOE *is talking to.*)

JORDAN. Okay.

JOE. (*To* TONY.) I—uh—look—I—I want a check.

TONY. Of course. (*He goes to desk, opens drawer.*) On what bank, sir?

JOE. Huh?

TONY. What bank? Chase, National City, Chemical, First Trust, Phoenix, Guaranty —— ?

JOE. Have I got money in all them banks?

TONY. (*Laughing.*) But, of course, sir.

JOE. Where have I got the most? This is a big check.

TONY. How big, sir?

JOE. (*Gulping.*) Twen—twenty —— (*The word "thousand" sticks in his throat a moment.*) —thousand!

TONY. You're joking.

JOE. (*To* MAX.) I guess it's too much—can't you fix it for less?

MAX. Not a cent less.

JOE. (*To* TONY, *doggedly.*) Twenty thousand is the amount;—maybe you'll have to make it out on four or five banks for all that dough?

TONY. Your account in each bank runs into hundreds of thousands, sir.

JOE. (*Staring at* TONY.) It does? Gee!

(MAX's *eyes go even wider than* JOE's.)

TONY. To whose order shall I draw the check?

JOE. (*Indicating* MAX.) To him.

TONY. The name, please.

MAX. (*Has a little difficulty getting the words out of his mouth.*) M-M-Max Levene.

JOE. (*To* TONY, *spells.*) L-E-V-E-N-E.

(*As* TONY *proceeds to write check,* JOE *still terribly worried about it, looks at* JORDAN, *who smiles assurance.* JOE *gulps.* TONY *finishes writing check.* MAX *mops his face.*)

TONY. (*To* JOE.) Will you sign it, please?

JOE. (*To* JORDAN, *worriedly.*) He wants me to sign it.

(TONY *again stares to see who* JOE *is talking to.*)

JORDAN. Go ahead!

JOE. (*Out of the corner of his mouth.*) I can get twenty years for this!

JORDAN. Sign it!

JOE. I'm in enough trouble already—if I get jammed up any more, I'll ——

JORDAN. You won't.

JOE. All right—you stand back of me. (*He goes over to desk—*TONY *rises and hands* JOE *the pen—*JOE *takes it and looks at* JORDAN, *who smilingly comes over; to* TONY.) How do you spell Farnsworth?

TONY. (*Laughing.*) Really, Mr. F.!

JOE. Go on—spell it!

TONY. (*A bit frightened.*) F-A-R-N-S-W-O-R-T-H!

JOE. (*To* JORDAN, *holding pen poised, nervously.*) I won't be able to ——

JOE. All right—here goes. (*As he writes,* MAX *comes over and looks over his shoulder.* JOE, *writing slowly, marvels at the ease with which it comes forth.*) Gee, it's rolling right out. (*He looks at it.*) I never wrote like this before. (*As he finishes signing check, he looks up fearfully at* TONY, *who looks at signature.*)

(*After a moment that seems an eternity to* JOE, TONY *blots check, tears it out and hands it to* MAX *who stares at it;* JOE *mops his brow in relief.*)

TONY. (*To* JOE.) Is that all?

JOE. Yes—that's all.

TONY. (*Starting out* L.) I hope you won't forget about the opening of the bridge, sir, and the Great Western board meeting at two?

JOE. Just don't worry about it.

TONY. Shall I wait here—or at the office?

JOE. The office—yeah, wait there.

TONY. Very well, sir. (*He exits* L.)

MAX. Look—suppose the bank finds out a ghost wrote this?

JOE. (*To* JORDAN.) How about that?

JORDAN. It's perfectly good.

JOE. If he says so, it's so, Max.

MAX. For twenty grand, I'll even take your friend's word for it. (*Pockets check.*)

(MRS. AMES *enters* L.)

MRS. AMES. Miss Logan calling, sir.

JOE. (*Excitedly.*) She is? Max, this is the girl I was tellin' you about —wait till you see her. Pretty as a sunset! (*To* MRS. AMES.) Don't stand there like a hitching post—bring her in as soon as the two gentlemen leave.

MRS. AMES. Yes, sir. (*Looking only at* MAX.) As soon as the *two* gentlemen leave. (*Exits* L.)

(JOE *hurries over to a mirror and hastily starts improving his appearance—straightening tie, slicks hair back, critically surveys himself.*)

JOE. Wait till you see her, Max. She's got plenty of zing—ain't she, Mr. Jordan?

(JORDAN *nods.*)

MAX. I better push along, Joe, and see what I can do.

JOE. Okay, Max—get that match set. As soon as I get the girl straightened out, I'm shedding Farnsworth.

MAX. What do you think you'll be next?

JOE. I don't know; I can be anybody. These fellows can do anything with you. I could even be War Admiral!

MAX. Who the hell wants to get up at five o'clock in the morning and run around a track? Say—here's an idea! (*Looking all around but chancing it.*) Mr. Jordan, how about making him Joe Louis? (*Laughs at his own joke.*)

JOE. Yeah—that's what I'm gonna hold out for—somebody like him.

MAX. (*A thought strikes him.*) Hey—wait a minute. I almost forgot. I got something to say about this, Joe. I got forty percent of you. I'll have to okay the change. Better tell Mr. Jordan I got to be in on the deal.

JOE. Yeah—he's right, Mr. Jordan.

MAX. Say—where are my brains? Why, I'm sitting pretty and I don't know it. Look, Joe, how much has Farnsworth got—cold cash?

JOE. About twenty million, I guess.

MAX. Whew! I'm rich! Forty percent of twenty million! Joe, we don't have to fight any more—we can ——

JOE. Now wait a minute, Max. This ain't permanent.

MAX. The whole goddam thing's got me screwy. I'm going out and get drunk. I'll call you as soon as I snap out of it. (*He has walked up to c. door.*) So long, Joe. (*Looking off into space.*) Er—can I drop you off some place? (*Pause.*) No? Okay. (*He salutes at nothing and exits L. JOE and JORDAN laugh.*)

JOE. (*To JORDAN, excitedly.*) Look, Mr. Jordan: you know everything—tell me, will—will she like me?

JORDAN. Very much, Joe.

JOE. But I don't want her to like Farnsworth. I want her to like me—Joe Pendleton.

JORDAN. (*Gently.*) I understand.

JOE. (*Glumly.*) Jeez—what a spot! I gotta make a girl hate the guy she can see and like the one she can't. How am I going to do it?

JORDAN. Don't worry about it, Joe. Here she comes. (*He quickly exits c.*)

(BETTE LOGAN *has entered L. and waits for* JOE *to see her.* JOE *turns and for the moment is speechless at sight of her. She misunderstands this and straightens up, ready for battle.*)

BETTE. Well—here I am!

JOE. (*Gulps.*) Hello, I—I'm sorry I couldn't talk to you last night when you were here, but ——

BETTE. (*Coldly.*) It's quite all right. Mrs. Farnsworth was good enough to let me know what you'd expect of me in return for helping my father. (*Grimly.*) Well—you win. I know how useless it would be to appeal to your sense of justice. I'll go away with you, but not until my father's completely cleared.

JOE. (*Distressed.*) Now, look, don't worry about your father. I promise ——

BETTE. (*Scornfully.*) You promise!

JOE. (*Earnestly.*) Look, Miss Logan, I'm your friend. I'm the best friend you've got. You don't know what I gave up just to meet you and help you.

(BETTE *stares curiously at him, puzzled by a new quality in his voice, and his earnestness.*)

43

JOE. You just wait and see. Is your father still in—jail?

BETTE. As if you don't know?

JOE. (*Angrily.*) This Farnsworth sure was a rat—but, gee, Miss Logan, I'm not like him—honest. (BETTE *stares at him.*) Why, I never gave anybody a wrong deal in my life, and I'm not going to start now. Look—you just tell me what to do and I'll do it.

BETTE. You mean that? You really mean that?

JOE. You bet I do.

BETTE. It's funny: you never talked like this before.

JOE. (*Takes a step nearer. She draws back, her eyes piercing his.*) That's because I'm a different guy now! I can't explain it, Miss Logan, and even if I did, you wouldn't believe me. (BETTE *is caught by his sincerity, and the look in his eyes. She feels herself impelled to listen. He continues.*) And about this trip—I mean about you going away with Farnsworth—that's out. You don't ever need to come here again or see him again. And I'll straighten out this business about your father right away.

BETTE. (*Puzzled, yet drawn to him somehow.*) I—I can't hope to understand what is in your mind; I—I don't know what has come over you.

JOE. If I told you you'd probably think I wasn't right in the head— you'd be afraid of me.

BETTE. (*Drawn irresistibly by a new and strange emotion.*) For the first time, I'm beginning not to be. I've seen you smile before and it always frightened me—but now—it seems so warm and friendly and gentle.

(JOE *takes a step nearer; this time she doesn't draw back.*)

JOE. I'm in an awful spot, Miss Logan. I *need* somebody like you. I'm lonesome—I haven't got *anybody*—I haven't even got *myself!*

BETTE. (*Staring strangely at him.*) I don't know why—but suddenly I feel warm and alive—and happy! There's a—sort of spiritual glow in your face that wasn't there before—and your eyes—as if—as if there was somebody inside them looking out!

JOE. That's *me* looking out, Miss Logan, but I ain't gonna be looking out for long; just until I get your father out of his jam—then I'm gonna be somebody else—somebody maybe you can like. (*He looks anxiously at her.*) Do—do you like fighters—professional fighters, I mean?

BETTE. (*Staring strangely at him.*) I don't know. I've never met one.

JOE. (*Grinning.*) Yes, you have. You've just met one—a pretty good

44

one, too—but you don't know it. Well, what I want to say is that some day—pretty soon now—some fighter will come up to you and say he knows you—and act like he's seen you before. Well, when he does, don't get sore—give him a chance—because he'll be telling you the truth, and he'll be a pretty good egg, and —— (*Floundering, as she stares wonderingly at him.*) What I'm trying to tell you is, now that I've met you, I don't ever want to lose you—and when I'm somebody else, I'll ——

(JULIA *and* TONY *enter* R.)

JULIA. Well, hello, Miss Logan, I suppose you and my husband have —— ?

JOE. *I'm not your husband!*

(*They* ALL *stare at him.*)

JULIA. Really, Jonathan —— !

JOE. *We're not married!*

JULIA. (*Aghast.*) What?

JOE. No, we're not—*not spiritually!*

(*As they gape at him,* MRS. AMES *enters* L.)

MRS. AMES. (*To* JOE.) The Chemical National Bank is on the phone, sir.

JOE. (*Panicky.*) Jeez! They know the check's phony! (*In a sweat, calls.*) Hey, Mr. Jordan—I'm in a jam—hey, Jordan!

(7013 *appears* C.)

7013. Can I be of service?

JOE. (*In disgust.*) No—not you—you'll gum me up again—get your boss here before I'm thrown in the can! (*Yells.*) Hey, Jordan—where the hell are you?

CURTAIN

ACT II

SCENE II: *The same.*

TIME: *A morning, three weeks later.*

AT RISE: MRS. AMES *and* SUSIE, *chambermaid, discovered.* MRS. AMES *holds a newspaper, reading it. She carries some very "loud" ties across her arm.*

45

MRS. AMES. Here it is, Susie, right on the front page.

SUSIE. Wha's it say?

MRS. AMES. Listen to this: (*Reads.*) "Financier Fights Killer Gilbert Tonight! Jonathan Farnsworth, Wall Street Tycoon, meets Killer Gilbert at Stadium in fifteen-round-go. American Carbide calls hurried Directors' meeting. Wall Street agog."

SUSIE. You mean he's actually going to fight in a ring like—like Joe Louis or somebody?

MRS. AMES. Yes, that's just it.

SUSIE. (*Grimly.*) Well, I'm not surprised after the things I've seen him do the past few weeks.

MRS. AMES. (*Sighs.*) From the Stock Exchange to the Stadium: from striped trousers to purple BVD's and these —— (*Indicates "loud" ties.*) —atrocities; from Oxford English to the slang of Jersey in one fell swoop. It's idiotic!

SUSIE. (*Excitedly.*) He's possessed, that's what he is. He's got devils inside him. A fighter and a musician each trying to get a stranglehold on him.

MRS. AMES. After listening to those saxophone solos, I'm rooting for the fistic demon to gain mastery.

SUSIE. All I know is, I'm getting out along with Cook in the morning, before I start talking to this "Mister Jordan" myself.

MRS. AMES. (*Looking at paper—musingly.*) I'm not a betting woman, as you know, but it seems to me there's what my dear husband used to call an inordinate overlay in the odds. Eight to one Farnsworth doesn't last the first round strikes me more as an excellent investment than a sordid wagering proposition. What do you say, Susie? Shall we take a flyer? My husband always wanted me to, but I didn't like to encourage him.

SUSIE. I don't want no part of it. Just when he gets in the ring, the musician is apt to get the upper hand and then where'll we be?

MRS. AMES. Hmmm! I hadn't thought of that. Still, eight to one, Susie. And from the way I've seen the master thump the bag, I'd say that the fistic demon within should easily manage to maintain supremacy over the decidedly third-rate musician.

SUSIE. You can't depend on devils, Mrs. Ames. (*She turns to confront another maid, ANN, who has entered without warning L. She jumps with fright.*) Ohhh! Don't come sneaking into rooms like that. Make a little noise when you come in.

ANN. Will Mr. Farnsworth see Mr. Levene in here?

MRS. AMES. Yes—hurry and have him come in. You know his orders.

46

(ANN *is out* L. *like a shot.*)

(MRS. AMES *looks down at the ties she is carrying only to cover her eyes and turn away with a shudder.*)

(MAX LEVENE *enters* L. *with an armful of newspapers.*)

MAX. (*To* MRS. AMES.) Where's Joe—er—I mean, Mr. Farnsworth?
MRS. AMES. In the study, Mr. Levene.
MAX. Study? You mean the bathroom, don't you? Go drag him out.
MRS. AMES. I'll tell him you're here. (*She starts out* R. *but stops and turns to* MAX.) I—I beg your pardon, Mr. Levene, but would you say Mr. Farnsworth has—well, a sporting chance in tonight's skirmish?
MAX. What do you mean—a chance? He's a cinch. Have yourself a little bet down.
MRS. AMES. I shall, sir. Thank you. (*She exits* R.)

(*The moment* MAX *is alone, he looks furtively around the room then, in a lowered voice, starts addressing a person he can't see.*)

MAX. Psst. Hey—Mr. Jordan—are you here? (*He stares all around—putting his hand behind his ear to catch a possible answer.*) Come on, Mr. Jordan. Give me a break. I got a sweet little deal I'll cut you in on if you'll play ball with me. (*He listens again.*) If you don't want to talk, just move a chair or something so I'll know you're around. (*He looks hopefully about to see if any furniture is moved but as nothing is, he gets a little peeved.*) Jeez, you're a tough guy to do business with. (*Suddenly a paper on the desk near the open door* C. *flutters into the air and on to the floor. He stops dead in his tracks.*) Is that you, Mr. Jordan? (*He looks fearfully behind him.*) Talk up, will you? After all, this ain't no comfortable position for a guy to be in. (*He looks about again, then.*) Okay, if that's the way you feel about it, but here's the deal: Here's Joe sitting pretty with twenty millions in the bank. He can get himself punched silly getting to be champ and what'll it get him? Certainly no twenty millions. Now, look, I'm a business man. I know what's best for Joe and after all, I got forty percent of him. He told me you can make him Mussolini or War Admiral or anybody—but *don't do it.* He's a pug and a little slap-happy and in case he suddenly wants to become Hitler, don't listen to him. That won't get him nothin'. (TONY *enters* R., *unseen by* MAX, *and stands listening to him as* MAX *continues talking and gesticulating.*) You've given him a swell deal. As his manager and forty

47

percent owner, I'm satisfied to have him stay Farnsworth, so don't go hunting up any more bodies for him.

TONY. Good morning, Mr. Levene.

MAX. (*Wheeling to face* TONY—*his face falls.*) Oh, it's you!

TONY. (*Coming toward him—dryly.*) Very interesting conversation.

MAX. (*Sourly.*) Yeah—but a little one-sided.

TONY. Mr. Farnsworth seems to have the same habit.

MAX. He gets results—I don't.

TONY. Just who is this mysterious Mr. Jordan that Mr. Farnsworth is constantly referring to?

MAX. (*Grimly.*) You'll find out. (JULIA *enters* R., *holding a small Pekinese dog.*) Good morning, Mrs. Farnsworth. Great day for the scrap, ain't it? They'll be hanging from the rafters—we're completely sold out. Look at the break I got him in the papers—front page! (*He brings a paper over to her.*) Listen to this: (*Reads.*) "Jonathan Farnsworth ——"

JULIA. (*Freezingly.*) I'm really not interested, Mr. Levene, in my husband's suddenly developed eccentricities.

MAX. That's too bad. He'd be tickled to death to see you in the *other* fellow's corner.

(MRS. AMES *enters* R.)

MRS. AMES. (*To* MAX.) Mr. Farnsworth has requested that you come up to his study.

MAX. (*Snorts.*) Still in there, eh? Why, the bum can't even read a telephone directory and he's "in his study." Where is it?

MRS. AMES. If you'll be good enough to follow me, sir.

JULIA. Mrs. Ames. (*Hands her the Pekinese.*) Have Ming Toy barbered.

MRS. AMES. Yes, ma'am. (*To* MAX.) This way, please. (MRS. AMES *exits* R.—MAX *follows her.*)

TONY. (*Picking up paper* MAX *left behind; to* JULIA.) You really should read this, my sweet—it puts the situation very neatly. (*Reads.*) "Wall Street's Problem Child. What will the spectacular J. F. do next? In the face of industry's collective howls for retrenchment, the financier declares his enterprises are making altogether *too much money* and proceeds to remedy the situation by ordering the *building of additional factories, doubling his payrolls and declaring quarterly bonuses for all his employees.* Not content with this generous nod toward the New Deal policies, he next offers to buy back at a premium the entire issue of the Logan Debentures despite

48

its worthlessness and the fact that John Logan is now languishing in the County Jail awaiting trial. And tonight he enters the professional arena seeking to ——"

JULIA. Stop it ——

TONY. (*Throwing paper aside.*) A few more weeks of this and you'll be a pauper, my sweet. Consolidated Steel, N.T. and Q Baylight and Power, are all being dumped on the market as fast ——

JULIA. Why haven't you stopped him?

TONY. Why haven't you? You've had ample opportunity.

JULIA. I haven't. He watches me like a hawk—constantly on his guard—constantly warning me—never alone with me for a moment. Even at night he ——

(JOE, *dressed in cap and turtle-necked sweater, comes trotting into the room* R. *He circles it at once and finishes off in a shadow-boxing exhibition.* MAX *saunters in and watches proudly.*)

MAX. Look at him—he's beautiful; watch that rhythm. I wish my car ran like that.

(JOE *finally stops as* JULIA *goes to him.*)

JULIA. Darling, surely you don't intend to go through with this— this preposterous fight ——

JOE. You bet I do—and if you're smart, you'll have yourself a little bet on me. (*Hotly.*) Imagine those clucks laying eight to one I don't last the first round. Why, I'll be on top of the Killer right from the bell. I'll even name the round that'll finish him. He's a sucker for a left hook.

MAX. Listen—you do just like I told you. Don't let him box you; you ain't got a chance boxing—he's got all that stuff pat. Coast! Wait for a chance and *sock!* You can take all he'll give you, but when you get in close, pick your spot and *hit*—and when you hit, HIT! The Killer's tough but you can drop him.

JOE. I'll say I can. Why, it'll be over in a minute! (*He swings a couple at an imaginary foe.*) I'll give him indigestion! I'll stop him same as I stopped Malone, which was no small-time stuff, if you'll remember, Max. That St. Louis cyclone was nobody's set-up. He had class, but I kept beating a tattoo on his lunch till his legs felt like they was made of spaghetti!

MAX. (*Impatiently.*) Yeah, yeah, come on—you gotta weigh in!

JOE. Yeah. (*He starts out* R.)

JULIA. Oh, just a moment, darling. I want to talk with you.

JOE. I ain't got time—I gotta go weigh in.

JULIA. Surely you can spare me a few moments?

JOE. I can't talk to anybody before a fight. I get upset. Don't I, Max?

(MAX *nods*.)

JULIA. This is more important than the fight.

JOE. Nothing's more important—not to me.

JULIA. Please, dear. (*To* TONY *and* MAX.) Will you excuse us? (*Holds out hand to* JOE.) Come along.

JOE. If you got anything to say, you can say it right here.

JULIA. But ——

TONY. (*Starting out* C.) If you'll excuse me —— (*To* MAX.) Shall we sit on the terrace, Mr. Levene?

JOE. Stay here, Max. (*To* JULIA.) Look—I got no secrets from Max. Go ahead—spill it—what's on your mind?

JULIA. It—it's rather personal, darling.

JOE. Then I don't want to hear it. Come on, Max. (*He starts out* C.)

JULIA. (*Taking his arm*.) Please—this is important to both of us. (*To* MAX.) I shan't keep him long.

TONY. (*Takes* MAX *by the arm and almost drags him out* C.) Come along.

JOE. (*Alarmed*.) Hey, Max, wait —— (*Starts to stop* MAX, *but* JULIA *comes quickly over to him and links her arm in* JOE's. TONY *and* MAX *exit* C.)

JULIA. You seem so afraid of being alone with me!

JOE. I'll say I am.

JULIA. But how silly, darling. Come —— (*Takes his arm and leads the reluctant* JOE *to divan*.) Sit here—close to me—for just a moment.

JOE. (*Drawing away*.) I—I ain't got time. I gotta weigh in—the Boxing Commission ——

JULIA. (*Pulling him down beside her*.) Darling, don't you think it's time we were honest with each other?

JOE. That's just what I want to be.

JULIA. Then don't avoid me. Let's talk it out straight from the shoulder—we can't go on like this.

JOE. We ain't going on. Right after this fight we're splitting.

JULIA. (*Dangerously*.) Are we?

JOE. Sure. We don't belong together.

JULIA. I'll never let you go, Jonathan. (*Suddenly* 7013 *appears* C. *As* JOE *stares at him*, 7013 *puts warning finger to his lips, indicating*

JULIA.) Despite this horrible change in you which I won't even try to understand, I still want you—I want you desperately. I love you.

(JOE *grimaces at* JULIA's *declaration and exchanges derisive looks with* 7013, JOE *registering a "get-this-lying-dame" expression.*)

JOE. Yeah—you love me—oh sure! I know I'm pretty dumb but not *that* dumb. You're nuts about Tony and he's nuts about you, which is okay with me because I'm going to marry Bette just as soon as I can fix it. I'm going to take it up with Mr. Jordan right after the fight. You'll soon be a widow like you wanted to be!

JULIA. (*Eyes narrowing.*) Shall I?

JOE. Yeah —— (*He rises—*JULIA *glares at him.*) —and don't try any funny business with me, either. You know what I mean. I'm on to you and the first wrong move you make, I'll hang one on your kisser—get me?

JULIA. (*Dangerously.*) Yes, my dear, I do! I'll be *very* careful —— (*Significantly.*) —next time. (*She exits* R.—JOE *looks after her a moment, then looks at* 7013.)

JOE. Imagine that dame!

7013. (*Beaming.*) You needn't worry about her, Mr. Pendleton. I bring good news.

JOE. Listen, you're just bad news to me.

7013. (*This is big and happy news and he is glad to impart it.*) Not this time. I've finally got what you've been asking for—a truly superb specimen—height, weight, chest expansion, biceps, reach, everything. You'll be delighted.

JOE. That's swell—but uh—is he—uh— (*A bit sheepishly.*) —good-looking?

7013. (*Surprised.*) I thought you were interested only in physical perfection.

JOE. (*Abashed.*) Yeah, sure I am—looks never meant anything to me before, only—well, now that I met Bette, I—I sort of want to look like somebody that won't be too hard on her eyes. He don't have to be a Clark Gable exactly—but somebody like him. You see, I can't afford to take any chances on her giving me the go-by. She's too important to my life!

7013. I see. Well, Mr. Pendleton, in that case, I'm afraid ——

(BETTE *enters* L.—*appears terribly worried.*)

BETTE. Jonathan ——

51

JOE. (*Smiling as he comes to her.*) Hello, honey; gee, I'm glad to see you. I was just on my way to the Stadium to weigh in—then I was going by your house and pick you up.

BETTE. Jonathan, I—I'm frightened!

(*7013 goes to divan and makes himself comfortable.*)

JOE. (*Patting* BETTE.) Aw, there ain't nothin' to be frightened about, honey. The fight's in the bag.

BETTE. It isn't the fight, dear. I can't shake off a feeling that—that somehow I'm going to lose you! (*She impulsively embraces him.*) Oh, Jonathan!

JOE. (*Laughing as he holds her close.*) Lose me? Not a chance, baby. I'm yours *for the next sixty years!* (*She looks wonderingly at him.*) Which reminds me—I know how long I'm gonna be around—but I gotta find out about *you.* (*Tenderly.*) I don't want to stay here a minute longer than you. (*Out of the side of his mouth to* 7013.) Better take care of that, Mr. Messenger.

BETTE. (*Smiling.*) Let's not worry about the future, dear—I—don't want to look too far ahead. I'm satisfied—just as things are.

JOE. (*Beaming.*) But they're gonna be better, honey—a lot better. There's going to be an important change in me.

BETTE. (*Looking worriedly at him.*) How do you mean, darling?

JOE. Remember what I told you about some day a fighter coming up to you and saying: "Hello, Bette," and acting like he's an old friend of yours?

BETTE. (*Puzzled.*) Yes.

JOE. Well, don't be surprised if that happens pretty soon now—right after your father's in the clear.

BETTE. Is this fighter a friend of yours?

JOE. (*Grins.*) I'll say he is—the best I got. (*Softly.*) Be nice to him, will you, honey? It's awful important!

BETTE. Of course, dear, only ——

JOE. (*Earnestly.*) I even want you to try to—to *more than like him!* (*As she looks wonderingly at him, he takes her face in his hands and stares hard.*)

BETTE. (*Worriedly.*) Why are you looking at me like that?

JOE. I gotta memorize your face. I gotta memorize everything about you, honey—so no matter what happens, I won't forget you! (*As she looks puzzled at him.*) Now, don't worry about a thing—we got a great life ahead of us! You see I got an "in" with a couple of big shots who'll make me anybody I want to be, so you just tell me what kind of a guy you'd like to marry if—if you had your choice—*and I'll be him!*

BETTE. (*Smiling.*) The kind of a guy you are, dear. Just as you are! Don't *ever* change!

JOE. (*Staring at her.*) You mean that? You really like me like I am—like this—like Farnsworth?

BETTE. (*With deep sincerity.*) I love you! I wouldn't want *anything* changed about you!

JOE. (*Amazed.*) And—you, you'd marry me the way I am? You'd marry Farnsworth?

BETTE. Of course—if I could, only ——

JOE. (*Elated.*) Sure you can, honey. Don't let Mrs. Farnsworth worry you. She don't mean a thing to me. I told her off just a few minutes ago—I told her we were all washed up right after the fight. She don't want me—she wants Tony.

BETTE. (*Quietly.*) Yes, I know.

JOE. (*Thrilled.*) So if you want me just as I am, *no changes,* why it's okay with me! And I'll tell the *boys* —— (*He looks significantly at* 7013.) —they can stop looking around for me—and get back to their jobs! *I'll keep Farnsworth and call everything square!*

(JOE *and* BETTE *embrace.* 7013 *grimaces.*)

7013. (*Annoyed.*) Oh, dear, I wish I'd known this earlier. I've been through hell trying to make good my error. (*Sigh.*) Well, Mr. Pendleton, I've done my part. I can report back now and say the matter is satisfactorily closed.

JOE. (*Happily.*) It sure is. And thanks for all you done for me!

7013. Don't mention it. (*Saluting* JOE.) Good luck to you, my boy! I'll pick you up in sixty years! (*He quickly exits* C., *passing* MAX, *who enters* C. *at the same moment.*)

MAX. (*Shuddering.*) Br-r! I just felt a cold chill! (*To* BETTE.) Hello, Miss Logan —— (*To* JOE, *as he looks suspiciously around room.*) Any of your "pals" around?

JOE. One of them just left. I'm through with them!

MAX. Good. Now let's get going before the Commissioners get the idea we're going to forfeit the fight.

JOE. Okay, Max—you take Bette down in the car—I'll go get my sax and be right with you.

MAX. Come on, Miss Logan.

BETTE. (*To* JOE.) Hurry, dear.

(*He smiles and nods.* BETTE *and* MAX *exit* L. *As* JOE *starts out toward* R., *the muted trumpet note of before sounds distantly and even before it is finished,* JORDAN'S *voice is heard, seemingly coming from the ceiling.*)

JORDAN'S VOICE. Wait, Joe!

(JOE *stops and looks up toward ceiling.*)

JOE. Oh, hello, Mr. Jordan. What's on your mind! I'm in a hurry.

JORDAN'S VOICE. I'm afraid I've some bad news for you.

JOE. I thought I was finished with you fellas. Didn't that Messenger tell you I was satisfied to call the whole thing square—that I'm gonna keep Farnsworth?

JORDAN'S VOICE. Yes, Joe! That's why I'm here. *You can't use Farnsworth's body any more!*

JOE. What?

JORDAN'S VOICE. I'm sorry, Joe, but he's been howling about it to the Registrar ever since you got into it.

JOE. (*Angrily.*) Oh, he has, eh? What's he got to squawk about?

(MAX *re-enters* L., *peeved.*)

MAX. I just telephoned the Boxing Commissioner and he said ——

JOE. I was just going when Mr. Jordan came in.

MAX. (*Staring around and seeing nobody—irked.*) Why don't you tell those fumble-bums to stop bothering you?

(JORDAN'S *laugh is heard.*)

JOE. I did.

MAX. What does he want?

JOE. He says I can't use Farnsworth's body any more.

MAX. (*Truculently.*) Does he expect you to fight without a body? Where is he? I'll talk to him.

JOE. (*Indicating.*) Up in the ceiling.

(MAX *stares up—flabbergasted.*)

MAX. Hey, look, Mr. Jordan—Joe's gotta tough fight on tonight and I don't want him upset.

JORDAN'S VOICE. *There isn't going to be any fight!*

JOE. (*Yells.*) What?

MAX. (*Anxiously.*) What did he say, huh, what did he say?

JOE. He said there wasn't going to be any fight!

MAX. (*Irked.*) He's nuts! We got twenty thousand bucks up!

JOE. (*To* JORDAN—*up in ceiling.*) What's the idea, Mr. Jordan?

JORDAN's VOICE. *Farnsworth objects!* He abhors pugilism!

(MAX *nearly goes crazy looking from* JOE *to ceiling, trying to hear what's being said.*)

MAX. (*Grabs* JOE.) What goes on here? Let me in on this!

JORDAN's VOICE. Tell Mr. Levene to call off the fight, Joe.

JOE. (*Angrily.*) Now, wait a minute, Mr. Jordan, wait a minute.

MAX. (*Irked as hell.*) What'd he say?

JOE. (*To* JORDAN.) You guys gummed me up enough. You put me in this spot and now I'm going to stay put, and you can tell Farnsworth ——

JORDAN's VOICE. Sorry, Joe, orders.

JOE. (*Grimly.*) Try to pry me loose!

MAX. Loose from what?

JOE. Never mind—come on, Max. (*He attempts to take a step forward, but finds it impossible to move. Again he tries—and fails.*) Something's holding me back! I can't move!

MAX. (*Irked.*) What do you mean you can't move? Come on! (*He tugs at* JOE, *but can't budge him.*) What's the matter—you nailed down?

JOE. (*Looks up at ceiling.*) Hey, cut the clowning, Mr. Jordan.

MAX. If he pulls a trick like that on you in the ring, you're a dead pigeon.

JOE. (*To* MAX.) You take Bette to the Stadium—tell the Commissioner I'll be a little late, but I'll be there! And I'll fight, tonight too! I'll settle this with Mr. Jordan!

MAX. I better stick around to protect my rights. (*He looks belligerently up at ceiling.*) Listen to me, Mr. Jordan—Joe and I are satisfied just as things are—Farnsworth suits us fine—we don't want no change, understand? Joe's been in training and he's got the guy's body in great shape ——

JOE. In the pink!

MAX. (*Continuing to* JORDAN.) So just forget the whole thing. We're not switching. And another thing—after this scrap, we're through with the fight game.

JOE. Like hell we are!

MAX. Look, Joe, I'm managing you, ain't I?

JOE. Yeah, sure you are, but ——

MAX. You know I won't steer you wrong. Take it from me—it's a lousy racket. All right, if you need the dough, but when a guy's got twenty million ——

JOE. (*Hotly.*) That's not my dough.

MAX. It's Farnsworth's, ain't it? And you're Farnsworth. And I got forty percent of whoever you are. I guess that gives me something to say.

JOE. Sure, Max, sure—but you forget I'm still Joe. I don't want any of that guy's coin. Bette and I are giving it back to the guys he swiped it from.

MAX. Are you nuts? Giving away twenty million sabaffles? Where do *I* come in?

JOE. You'll make plenty with me. Just keep getting me fights. I got to get to be champ—so I can ask Bette to marry me. I can't do that till I'm making enough to support her.

MAX. (*Ready to tear his hair.*) Listen to him—he's got twenty millions and he's worrying about supporting a wife.

JOE. Gotta work this out by myself, Max. You get over to the Stadium and I'll join you and Bette as soon as I have it out with —— (*He looks up at ceiling.*) —him.

MAX. But ——

JOE. Do like I tell you. You can't talk to Mr. Jordan and you can't see him—so you can't help me!

MAX. (*Reluctantly.*) Well, all right, Joe—but stand pat—understand? Don't jeopardize my interests.

JOE. Leave it to me, Max.

MAX. Okay. (*He looks disgustedly up at ceiling.*) You're a fine guy to do business with. (*He exits* L.)

JOE. (*As he looks up at ceiling.*) Now, Mr. Jordan —— (JORDAN *suddenly appears from behind a large chair* U.C.) —let's you and me get this thing settled for keeps.

JORDAN. (*Gently.*) It's not up to me, my boy. (*Surprised that* JORDAN's *voice no longer comes from ceiling,* JOE *whirls to face him.*) There's no reasoning with Farnsworth. He's as difficult up there as he was down here.

JOE. What's he bellyaching about? I was taking better care of his body than he did; I got it in swell shape. He ought to be tickled.

JORDAN. He doesn't like what you're doing with his money—giving it away—that seems to hurt him even now!

JOE. What good is it to him, the big no-good crook? Listen, Mr. Jordan, that louse never made an honest nickel in his life. He ought to be in jail instead of where he is! Why, it'll take me the next five years to square things for him.

JORDAN. All that will be adjusted, Joe. You've got to get back on your own road. All mankind has its own particular beam of light—its place in the sun. This is not for you, my boy.

JOE. Oh, I ain't doin' so bad. In a month or so, I'd get the hang of things and show those big shots on the Street what to do with money. I'd show them how to spread it around so everybody would get a break.

JORDAN. Sorry, Joe. This arrangement cannot stand.

JOE. Now, look, I don't want any more trouble with you boys. I'm sticking to Farnsworth and that's that. I'm not letting you play tricks with my life again.

JORDAN. (*Kindly.*) On the contrary, Joe, I want to clear it up for you.

JOE. Just leave it alone! It's okay as is! Bette loves me as Farnsworth and that's how it's going to be. I'm taking no chances. I had a tough time getting her to love the rat.

JORDAN. You are no more able to stop the course of what's to be than you can stem the waves of the sea with your hand, or stay the sun in the midst of heaven.

JOE. (*Truculently.*) No—well, just let somebody separate me from Farnsworth and see what happens. (*Suddenly a hand thrusts its way through the curtains* U.C. *holding a gun, which points at* JOE's *back as he starts out.*) Goodbye, Mr. Jordan. (*The gun explodes.* JOE *is shot. His eyes open—AS IF WITHOUT PAIN BUT IN WONDERMENT. He staggers to divan; angrily.*) Who was it? Who got me? I'll bet it was Mrs. Farnsworth! Call the cops—no, never mind—I'll call them myself. (*He starts for phone on desk.*) Hello—police ——

JORDAN. (*Kindly.*) Don't fight, Joe. *Leave Farnsworth!*

(JOE *has been standing behind divan; now he weakly crumples but with no sign of pain, and disappears behind divan.*)

(MESSENGER 7013 *appears at door* C.)

7013. (*Sourly.*) Good Lord, have I got him on my hands again?

CURTAIN

ACT III

TIME: *About 9.00 P.M. A week later.*

AT RISE: POLICE INSPECTOR WILLIAMS *is in the midst of an investigation concerning the mysterious disappearance of* FARNSWORTH. *Seated around the room are* JULIA, TONY, BETTE *and* MAX. *One of the* INSPECTOR's *men, a* PLAINCLOTHESMAN, *stands nearby.*

WILLIAMS. Now look, I'm a conscientious fellow—I haven't got an ounce of imagination—the only way I break a case is to cover every possible angle, collect all facts, that's the way I work—methodically —that's why I've got to know everything Mr. Farnsworth did last Friday, the day he disappeared—what he ate for breakfast; what he said; how he slept the night before; I even want to know whether he cleaned his teeth that particular morning—everything. Little facts point big fingers. So, let's start all over again. (*To* JULIA.) Mrs. Farnsworth, I wish you'd ——

JULIA. (*Sullenly.*) I've already told you all I know.

WILLIAMS. (*Coaxingly.*) Tell me again—maybe I missed something —or maybe somebody *forgot* something.

MAX. You're going to find this the damnedest case you ever tackled. (WILLIAMS *glares at him.*) You'll never crack it without you call in a spiritualist.

WILLIAMS. (*Glaring at him.*) Will you shut up? (*To others.*) Everything has been checked and cross-checked—every morgue, hospital, rooming-house, hotel, railroad, steamship and airline has been covered—nothing has been overlooked—and yet there's not a single trace—even the large reward has brought no clue of him to light.

(MAX *gets up and starts walking around, looking behind furniture, in piano, behind curtains, whispering.*)

MAX. Psst! Hey, Joe—you here? Hey, Joe, for Pete's sake, where are you? Who are you *now?* Come on—give me a break.

WILLIAMS. What the hell are you doing?

58

MAX. Looking for Joe.

WILLIAMS. Who's Joe?

MAX. He may be anybody—I don't know. (*Continues his search.*) Hey, psst, Joe —— (*To* PLAINCLOTHESMAN.) Hey, are you Joe? Hey, Joe, Joe!

PLAINCLOTHESMAN. Maybe we'd better call the psychopathic.

(*At this moment* JULIA'*s little Pekinese trots into the room* C. MAX *looks at it wide-eyed—then in an undertone to dog.*)

MAX. Hey, Joe ——

(JULIA *grabs dog and puts him in her lap. As* MAX *comes over and stares at it.*)

WILLIAMS. Levene, are you going to sit down?

MAX. Not till I find Joe—or his pal Jordan.

WILLIAMS. Who's Jordan?

MAX. He's the guy who put Joe in Farnsworth's body!

WILLIAMS. (*Disgusted.*) Oh, sit down!

MAX. I'm afraid to sit down—I may be sitting on Joe. (*He goes to a chair, brushes it off and sits.*)

WILLIAMS. (*To* BETTE.) Miss Logan, you and Mr. Levene were sitting in Mr. Farnsworth's car outside the house waiting for him?

BETTE. (*Broken-heartedly.*) Yes.

WILLIAMS. You were going to the stadium to see him weigh in for his fight with Gilbert?

BETTE. Yes.

WILLIAMS. And you never saw or heard from him since?

BETTE. (*On point of tears.*) No.

WILLIAMS. (*To* MAX.) Now, you, when you last saw him, what was he doing?

MAX. Arguing with some guy from Heaven!

WILLIAMS. (*Savagely.*) That's just what you'll be doing if you don't cut the clowning!

MAX. You'll be as nuts as I am after you're on this case a couple of days.

WILLIAMS. Mrs. Farnsworth, I needn't point out to you —— (*To* BETTE.) —nor to you, Miss Logan, how important it is for you to help me.

TONY. (*To* JULIA.) Tell the Inspector everything, Mrs. Farnsworth, you've nothing to fear. (*He pats her hand reassuringly.*) *Not a thing.*

JULIA. (*To* WILLIAMS.) I can only repeat that my husband's disappearance is neither mysterious, nor does it surprise me in the least. Not in view of his actions for several weeks previous. His conviction that he was a fighter—giving away his money ——

BETTE. (*Defensively.*) He wasn't giving it away, he was making restitution.

TONY. Restitution? Farnsworth? Really, Miss Logan, I don't think you quite knew him!

BETTE. I knew him better than any of you; he was fine, good, lovable.

JULIA. (*To* BETTE.) You can't possibly be referring to my husband, Miss Logan.

(BETTE *flashes her an angry look.*)

(JOE *and* MESSENGER 7013 *enter* C.; *no one, of course, sees or hears them.*)

(7013 *goes to piano and sits, while* JOE *eagerly goes to* BETTE *and stands behind her chair.*)

(BETTE *begins to sob,* JOE *is terribly affected.*)

JOE. Don't cry, honey. I'll be back with you!

WILLIAMS. (*To* JULIA.) When you last talked to your husband, was your interview friendly? No quarrel of any kind?

JULIA. It was—amicable.

WILLIAMS. How do you mean that?

JULIA. He told me he loved Miss Logan. (BETTE *sobs softly.*) That he wanted to marry her—and wanted a divorce.

JOE. (*To* WILLIAMS *who, of course, doesn't see or hear him.*) I guess that's why she shot me.

WILLIAMS. I see . . . Ummmm!

MAX. You can say "Ummm" again, but it won't get you a thing!

WILLIAMS. Miss Logan, if Mr. Farnsworth is alive, you feel sure he'd communicate with you?

BETTE. I *know* he would.

JOE. (*To* BETTE.) You bet I would, Honey.

JULIA. Perhaps he's lost interest, my dear. Another pretty face—I told you Jonathan was like that!

BETTE. (*Hysterically.*) He was murdered! I'm sure of it!

JOE. (*To* WILLIAMS.) She's telling you right, Inspector.

TONY. I believe Mr. Farnsworth wanted to create exactly that impression; you see, certain rather ominous transactions, particularly the Gulf Oil project, bear out my belief that Mr. Farnsworth chose to mysteriously *disappear* rather than face possible investigation.

BETTE. That's a lie!

JULIA. (*Purringly to* BETTE.) If, as you say, he's been murdered, where is his body?

JOE. (*To* JULIA.) It's in your trunk!

TONY. (*Banteringly to* BETTE.) Of course, Mrs. Farnsworth could have cut it up, stuffed it in a trunk, flown it out over the Atlantic, and ——

BETTE. (*Tortured.*) Stop it! Stop it! (*Sobs.*)

JOE. (*To* 7013.) Hey, they're killing Bette—I can't stand it. What's keeping Jordan so long?

7013. He's in conference with the Registrar trying to get you straightened out.

JOE. He's been in conference a whole week. How long does he think I can run around without a body?

7013. Patience, Mr. Pendleton, patience.

(MAX *starts pacing.* 7013 *sits at piano and softly idles on keys.*)

MAX. This thing's got me screwy. I use every trick I know to get him matched with the "Killer"; I get thrown out of every newspaper office in town before I convince them I'm managing Farnsworth. I run my goddam can off; I don't sleep nights; I don't eat, and what do I wind up with—forty percent of a ghost—forty percent of nothing. And I can't even find that.

JOE. I'm sorry, Max.

MAX. (*To* WILLIAMS.) Look, you think you're looking for Farnsworth, but you're really looking for Joe. *Farnsworth's dead!*

BETTE. (*Agonized.*) I knew it—I knew it!

(ALL *stare at* MAX.)

MAX. He was drowned in the bathtub by his wife and that guy there —— (*Indicates* TONY.) —*three weeks ago.*

JULIA. (*Springs up as if shot—staring at* MAX.) You're mad!

MAX. You bet I am—I'm madder'n hell. Why shouldn't I be? I've been all over this town looking for Joe. I've been out to the racetrack, the zoo, and the aquarium. I've asked every horse, monkey and fish if they were Joe.

TONY. Get hold of him, Inspector, he's apt to get violent.

61

(WILLIAMS *signals to* PLAINCLOTHESMAN, *who comes over and grabs* MAX.)

MAX. (*Fighting to get loose.*) Let go of me, flatfoot! (*He tries to shake him off.*)

WILLIAMS. Hold on to him, Mike!

(*As they struggle,* BETTE *starts sobbing afresh.*)

JOE. (*To* 7013.) Jeez, I can't stand here and watch Bette cry. Come on!

7013. Where?

JOE. Up to your joint! I'm going to have it out with the Registrar myself!

7013. It's not the Registrar that's holding you up, Joe. It's Farnsworth!

JOE. (*Grimly.*) We'll see about that! Come on!

7013. Very well.

(*As they start out* C. JOE *stops.*)

JOE. Wait a minute—I'll be right back! (*He rushes out* C.)

WILLIAMS. (*To* MAX, *sarcastically.*) So Mr. Farnsworth was drowned in his bathtub, was he?

MAX. Yeah.

WILLIAMS. Three weeks ago?

MAX. Right.

WILLIAMS. And he's only been missing a week!

MAX. (*Struggling to free himself.*) I don't care. That's what he told me.

WILLIAMS. Who told you?

MAX. Joe—I mean Farnsworth.

WILLIAMS. Just when did he tell you this, before or *after* he was drowned?

MAX. *After!*

WILLIAMS. (*To* PLAINCLOTHESMAN.) Take him down to the psycho-pathic—quick. (*As* PLAINCLOTHESMAN *starts to drag him out* L., *a piercing scream is heard off-stage; it startles everybody.*) Come on ——

(*As* WILLIAMS *starts rushing out of the room* R., *everybody goes after him, that is, everybody but* 7013, *who goes to piano again, and starts playing. After a moment,* JOE *returns* C. *carrying his saxophone.*)

7013. What was the screaming about?

JOE. I don't know. It's that crazy maid. Come on!

(7013 *finishes a few notes; then starts out* C. *with* JOE; *at* C. *door they suddenly bump into* JORDAN.)

JORDAN. (*Smiling.*) Where are you going, boys?

JOE. Oh, so you finally got back—I've been waiting all week for you —what's the idea of leaving me like this? What's the —— ?

JORDAN. (*Interrupting.*) I've been busy with Mr. Farnsworth.

JOE. Did that take all week?

JORDAN. I had my other duties to take care of, Joe. (*Curtly, to* 7013.) Report back!

7013. Yes, sir. (*Salutes and exits* C.)

JOE. Now, look. Never mind your other duties. Get *me* straightened out first.

JORDAN. Patience, my boy. I've prevailed upon the Registrar to intercede for you. Undoubtedly, he'll win Farnsworth over—he has more persuasive powers than I have. Don't worry about it, Joe! I promise you, you shan't be cheated—everything will be accounted for in the final reckoning.

JOE. Yeah—by the time you fix me up I'll be due at your place.

JORDAN. You'll live your full life, Joe. That can't be denied you.

JOE. All I want is Bette—fix that and I'll call the whole thing square.

JORDAN. I expect a flash any moment. If it's favorable, you'll be Farnsworth again.

JOE. Is the body still in good condition?

JORDAN. Excellent—it's in a refrigerator at the moment.

JOE. Jeez, get me out of there—I'll freeze to death!

(JORDAN *laughs. The crowd comes back* R., SUSIE *and* MRS. AMES *are now in the group.*)

SUSIE. (*Hysterically.*) I tell you I saw it with my own eyes—I was cleaning the master's room and I just got around to wiping off his saxophone when somebody or something snatched it out of my hand, and it went sailing out of the room!

WILLIAMS. You're crazy!

MAX. (*Excitedly.*) No—she ain't—that was Joe—he's here ——

(*He spies saxophone which* JOE *has placed on piano, rushes over and grabs it.*)

JOE. Hey—let that alone!

MAX. Look—his saxophone!

WILLIAMS. What of it?

MAX. It wasn't here before. I tell you Joe's in this room with us! (*Calls.*) Hey, Joe—where are you? Who are you? Come on, let Max know. Say something. I'm going screwy!

WILLIAMS. (*Savagely.*) So am I! Now sit down and let's get on with this investigation.

JOE. I was supposed to take Bette to see the big fight tonight—Murdock and Smallings—but I can't take her without a body!

JORDAN. You can see the fight if you wish to, Joe!

JOE. I don't want to go without her!

JORDAN. Would you care to hear it?

JOE. Sure. How?

JORDAN. The radio. It's on the air now—they've just started.

JOE. Gee, I hate to miss it. Wish one of those clucks would tune in. Here's the biggest fight of the year going on and they're wasting their time trying to find me!

JORDAN. Mr. Levene will turn it on if you concentrate on him.

JOE. Yeah? (JORDAN *nods.*) All right, I'm concentrating. Come on, MAX. (*Suddenly leaps up and looks at his watch.*) Holy smoke, it's ten o'clock! The fight's on ——⌐ (*He hurries to radio and tunes it in. Various stations come over—music, singing, dance band, news flashes—then the fight broadcast. Announcer's excited voice comes over.*)

INSPECTOR. (*To* MAX.) What did you do that for? Max, turn on the radio.

MAX. (*Shrugs shoulders.*) I don't know. I had to.

JOE. (*To* JORDAN, *smiling.*) It worked. Can you get people to do things you want them to do just by concentrating?

JORDAN. (*Smiling.*) It depends on what you want them to do, Joe.

WILLIAMS. (*To* MAX, *irately.*) Turn that off!

ANNOUNCER'S VOICE. (*Excitedly.*) Now Murdock is crowding Smallings to the ropes —— (*The frenzied roar of crowd is heard.*) Murdock shoots over a right cross, a left jolt to the chin, Smallings' eye is swelling —— (*Again the crowd.*) Murdock whips over a left, a right, another left to Smallings' jaw—all powerful blows that hit their mark with the speed and accuracy of a bullet. Smallings lands one on Murdock's eye but it glances off—Murdock comes back with a right cross, a left jab, then sends a hammer-fisted jab to Smallings' chin ——

(*During this excited report, everybody forgets the investigation and starts crowding around radio, listening eagerly.*)

(NOTE: *The stage is suddenly darkened save for two pools of light shining down on* JOE *and* JORDAN.)

JOE. (*Enthusiastically.*) Murdock is dynamite—I know his style like a book—always keeps that left curled up over his chest like it's asleep; then suddenly, wham! He lets fly.

JORDAN. (*Smiling.*) I thought you said he was just a "palooka"—that he couldn't hit the side of a house?

JOE. (*Gulping.*) Well—yeah—he—he's just lucky tonight, I guess.

ANNOUNCER'S VOICE. (*Terrific excitement.*) Smallings isn't in this at all. Murdock's doing just as he pleases with him—he jolts Smallings with a short right, rips over a left to the ribs which unbalances Smallings. Infuriated, Smallings swings wildly but can't touch Murdock. Now Murdock crowds Smallings to the ropes sending in the most punishing blows a man's ever taken —— (*As a veritable bedlam of noises, the furious, uncontrollable roar of crowd comes over.*) Smallings is down—from a smashing blow to the head that lifted him clear off his feet—he looks finished—lying there completely limp as the referee counts ——

REFEREE'S VOICE. Two—three—four ——

JORDAN. (*Teasingly.*) That can't be *all* luck, Joe.

JOE. Sure it is. He's got a setup. Smallings is a pushover!

JORDAN. Murdock's a great fighter, Joe, and you know it. In your heart, you admire and respect him very much. You'd even *like to be like him!*

JOE. (*Unconvincingly.*) Who? Me? Be like Murdock? Don't make me laugh!

REFEREE'S VOICE. (*Continuing.*) —eight—nine ——

ANNOUNCER'S VOICE. He's up! Smallings is up! Murdock rushes over—they exchange a few harmless blows —— (*Deafening roar comes over.*) Now *Murdock* is down! He's down—he's flat on the floor—from what seemed a harmless tap on the side of the head—hardly strong enough to throw him. But Murdock went down like a shot ——

JOE. (*Triumphantly.*) There—what'd I tell you? Just a palooka like I always said!

JORDAN. Listen!

ANNOUNCER'S VOICE. The referee is bending over Murdock—nobody can understand it—he must have taken suddenly ill—it certainly wasn't the blow Smallings delivered—it couldn't be ——

JOE. Jeez, I wonder what happened? He was going like a buzz saw ——

JORDAN. *He's dead,* Joe!

JOE. (*Gapes at him.*) What? You're crazy! You heard him knocking Smallings around like he was a tenpin. Why, he's got a physique like a solid chunk of rubber, a chest like an Indian's backside, a pair of arms like ——

JORDAN. *He was shot*—he's got a bullet in his heart—he was told to throw the fight—and he refused.

JOE. (*Incensed.*) Why, the dirty, slimy skunks—knockin' off a swell guy like Murdock. Didn't they hear that shot?

JORDAN. Not with all that noise.

REFEREE'S VOICE. —four—five—six ——

JOE. Jeez—they're counting over a dead man! Can't they tell?

JORDAN. They won't know until after he's counted out.

JOE. (*A lump in his throat.*) Poor Murdock—they didn't come no better. A clean fighter, a swell guy—a credit to the game. You were right, Mr. Jordan, how I really felt about him. Jeez—*he was my idol!*

JORDAN. (*Kindly.*) Of course he was, Joe. But his job was done. Everybody goes when that's done; and the job may be only to have dreamed a few notes of music—for a baby to have romped in the park and laugh happily; for lovers to have had one perfect day— that is enough to die on.

JOE. (*Blazing.*) I'd like to get those guys. They're what give the game a black eye! Jeez—I wish I could do something, Mr. Jordan. I—I wish I could be in there finishing the fight for him. *I'd like to be him for just five minutes!*

JORDAN. (*Quietly.*) You can, Joe.

JOE. (*Stares at him.*) Yeah? You mean —— ?

JORDAN. We've got just one second to make it, Joe!

JOE. Come on —— (*Lights come on full again as* JOE *grabs saxophone.*) Wait, Bette—I'll be right back!

(SUSIE *sees saxophone lifted; screams.*)

SUSIE. (*Pointing.*) There it goes again!

(ALL *stare in direction of* SUSIE'S *finger.* JOE *and* JORDAN *rush out* C.; ANNOUNCER'S VOICE *comes over.*)

ANNOUNCER'S VOICE. —eight—nine —— (*Suddenly very excited.*) *Murdock is up!* He leaped up like a rocket—full of fight! It's amazing! He was lying there like a dead man and now he's on his feet! Smallings rushes him and is met by a staggering right from Murdock—a left—a right—another left —— Smallings rocks dizzily—Murdock jabs his left to Smallings' chin and down he goes! Now, *Smallings is down* —— (*The bell sounds.*) And there goes the bell saving Smallings from what looked like a sure knock-out. What a fight! What a comeback for Murdock! He looked finished and suddenly comes up like a dynamo —— Ladies and gentlemen, this battle will go down in history as the most sensational encounter of all time!

(MAX *starts out.*)

WILLIAMS. Levene! Where are you going?
MAX. I'm following that saxophone! (*And he rushes out.*)

CURTAIN

ACT III

SCENE II: *A dressing room underneath the Stadium. There are a couple of rubbing tables, a long wooden bench, some lockers and a few hooks on which hang pieces of clothing. A door L. leads to showers; a door R. to the arena. The room is dimly lit because of one or two light bulbs which are burned out.*

AT RISE: *The stage is empty. Through the open door the roar of the crowd, now subdued, now raised in frenzy comes through. Throughout this scene the distant roars and intermittent clang-ing of bell continue.*

The above description of the set can, of course, be followed literally, but it is suggested that only one rubbing table be used and that lockers and hooks be left to the imagination. The same thing is true of the doors, which can be imagined as off-stage.

(*An* OLD, BENT MAN [*Really* MR. JORDAN, *but now not recognizable*] *hobbles in carrying a few light bulbs. He proceeds to fix lights,*

67

working in the darker part of the room, his back to audience so that his face is only vaguely seen. OLD MAN *continues work for a moment, then hobbles out, almost colliding with the group entering with the flushed and triumphant* JOE *in their midst. The group is made up of* LEFTY, *Murdock's manager; his trainer, a handler, and a few enthusiastic friends.*)

(JOE *goes over to rubbing table, perches on it; throws off his robe while* LEFTY *starts removing his gloves and cutting tape on his hands.*)

LEFTY. (*Enthusiastically, to* JOE.) You put up the greatest fight of your life, K. O. Jeez, just as I was thinking you was a goner you jump up like a rocket on the count of nine. I'm proud of you.

JOE. Thanks. This guy Murdock is the best.

LEFTY. (*Enthusiastically.*) I'll say you are!

JOE. No—I don't mean me—I said *Murdock!*

LEFTY. (*Laughing.*) Say it any way you like. You're champ now—that's all that matters.

JOE. Poor Murdock—I hope he's happy I did this for him.

(LEFTY *and the others look queerly at him.* LEFTY *goes off a second and returns, carrying* JOE's *saxophone.*)

LEFTY. (*To* JOE.) Hey, K. O.—look what they found under your stool.

(JOE *leaps off table, runs over to him and grabs saxophone.*)

JOE. Give me that.

LEFTY. Whose is it?

JOE. Mine!

LEFTY. Since when did you play a sax?

JOE. I always play it.

LEFTY. I never heard you. You musta been practicing in secret. How'd it get in the ring? You didn't have it when you climbed in. There's something goddam funny about this—I don't get it—I don't get you, either, K. O. Come on—we're pals—we never hid anything from each other—tell me what the hell's got into you? You're feeling all right, ain't you?

JOE. Sure. I feel swell.

LEFTY. (*Looking at him.*) There's a funny, faraway look in your eye I don't like. What are you thinking about?

JOE. Poor K. O. Murdock!

LEFTY. Cut it out, will you?

JOE. (*More to himself.*) He won the fight—he's champ!

LEFTY. (*Puzzled.*) Sure you're champ, and we're all set to clean up.

JOE. Hang on to the dough. You ain't going to make much more.

LEFTY. You're crazy. Here's where we start making the big money.

JOE. K. O. Murdock's through.

LEFTY. (*Now terribly worried about* JOE's *talk and manner.*) What are you talking about? Why, you're perched on top of the world.

JOE. I ain't perched any place. I don't know *where* I go from here.

LEFTY. I do—nothing can stop you now, K. O., but I don't mind telling you, I'm glad it's over. I was pretty worried.

JOE. I wasn't.

LEFTY. Oh, I didn't mean that you wouldn't win. Hell, that was in the bag all the time. I mean, about those gorillas—remember what they told you—I was scared stiff they were going to pull something funny.

JOE. (*Grimly.*) They did—and it wasn't funny! They shot Murdock. Look! (*Throws off his robe, disclosing a wound near his heart.*)

LEFTY. (*Staring at it; gasps.*) Holy cats! No wonder you're talking delirious. Come on—lie down—take it easy —— (*To others.*) Watch him, boys—till I get the Doc.

(*He rushes out.* A CROWD *at the door clamors to come in. They come over to* JOE, *but he pushes them back.*)

JOE. Go on—scram! I'm all right.

(MAX *enters excitedly. He looks at "Murdock," then spies saxophone in* JOE's *hand and rushes over to him.*)

MAX. Where'd you get that sax, Murdock? (*Tries to wrest it away.*)

JOE. (*Holding fast to sax.*) Jeez, Max—you *never* know me!

(MAX *stares hard at* JOE; *then at saxophone, then comes very close to* JOE, *almost trembling. He feverishly starts feeling* JOE's *arms, legs, head; then gulps.*)

MAX. Are—are you?

JOE. (*Grins.*) Yeah, Max! Sure—I am!

(*The others stare from* MAX *to* JOE, *unable to grasp it.*)

MAX. (*Yells joyfully.*) Joe! (*Hugs him, almost sobbing.*) Joe

69

——!! (*Then quickly breaks away and gets angry.*) What are you doing in Murdock's body? Come on—get out of it!

(*Enter* LEFTY. *Stops, amazed.*)

LEFTY. What kind of screwy talk is that, Levene?

LEVENE. I'm lucky I'm able to talk at all.

JOE. Take it easy, Max. I just took Murdock's body to help him out!

MAX. Help *me* out, will you? Stop jumping from body to body! Stay put!

JOE. Sure, but you see, Max, a bunch of gorillas shot Murdock and ——

LEFTY. (*To* MAX.) K. O.'s delirious, Levene. He's got a bullet in him! Where's the Doctor? He was following me —— (*Turns to look for him.*)

MAX. Where? Let's see.

JOE. (*Opening robe.*) It don't bother me!

MAX. (*Stares at wound.*) A fine body you got into.

LEFTY. (*To* JOE—*soothingly.*) The Doc'll be here right away, K. O.—just lie down and keep quiet—and you'll be all right. (*Tries to get* JOE *to lie down, but he angrily shoves him away.*)

JOE. Beat it, you. There ain't nothin' wrong with me!

LEFTY. (*Calling off.*) Hey, Doc! This way!

MAX. I'll need that Doc, too.

JOE. Everything will be okay as soon as Jordan gets here.

(DOCTOR *enters.*)

LEFTY. Here he is, Doc ——

(DOCTOR *goes to* JOE.)

MAX. How's your heart, Lefty?

LEFTY. (*Snaps.*) I ain't got any.

MAX. You're lucky. I was just going to break it.

LEFTY. You got no business here, Levene.

MAX. (*Grimly.*) That's what you think!

JOE. (*To* DOC.) Scram, Doc. I don't need you. Go on—go home.

LEFTY. Be reasonable, K. O. You got a bullet in you, ain't you?

JOE. (*Snaps.*) How many times I have to tell you *Murdock* got the bullet!

LEFTY. (*To* DOC.) Examine his head, too—he's out of it!

DOCTOR. (*Soothingly—to* JOE.) Just let me have a look at the wound.

JOE. Okay—but don't go taking it out until after I'm out of this body!

DOCTOR. (*Staring at him.*) You intend to leave this body?

JOE. Yeah—I don't belong in it!

LEFTY. (*Wails.*) Holy Rockabye, K. O., don't talk like that! Please! Doc, *do* something!

(DOCTOR *continues examining* JOE.)

MAX. (*Grimly—to* LEFTY.) Well, *partner!*

LEFTY. I wouldn't be partners with you in an unborn flea!

MAX. I'm laughing!

LEFTY. Get out of here, Levene, I got enough trouble.

MAX. Don't be so optimistic!

LEFTY. Aw, you're nuts!

MAX. You're giving me information.

(WILLIAMS *and* PLAINCLOTHESMAN *enter.*)

WILLIAMS. (*To* MAX—*truculently.*) Now, Levene, what about that saxophone you were following?

MAX. Here it is, and —— (*Indicating* JOE.) —*there's the body you're looking for!*

WILLIAMS. (*Looks at* JOE—*sarcastically.*) Oh, it is?

MAX. Yeah—he's Farnsworth!

WILLIAMS. Oh, he is?

JOE. Yeah—only I'm not using Farnsworth's body now!

WILLIAMS. Whose body *are* you using?

JOE. Murdock's, but I'm really Joe Pendleton!

(LEFTY *tears his hair.*)

WILLIAMS. And who am I?

MAX. (*To* WILLIAMS.) Jesse James.

JOE. Could be!

LEFTY. Don't pay any attention to Murdock, Inspector. He was just shot—the doc's probing for the bullet now. (*To* DOC.) Find it yet, Doc?

DOCTOR. Yes—it's in his heart!

LEFTY. (*In terror.*) Holy Hell!

DOCTOR. (*To* JOE.) Why aren't you dead?

JOE. (*Simply.*) I was once—for a while—wasn't I, Max?

71

MAX. He sure was, because *I cremated his body!*

WILLIAMS. (*This is too much—flings hat to floor.*) Goddammit, will *somebody* talk *sense* around here?

JOE. Aw, you just don't understand.

MAX. (*In disgust.*) Cops are just a bunch of Gracie Allens!

WILLIAMS. (*Furious.*) Listen, Levene ——

MAX. Just keep still, and I'll clear up the Farnsworth case for you. (*To* JOE.) Go ahead—tell the Inspector what happened.

WILLIAMS. Yeah—tell me.

JOE. Don't go wasting any time on Farnsworth. Get after the lugs who knocked Murdock off. Farnsworth will be okay just as soon as I get him out of the ice-box and get into him. I'll invite you all to his wedding!

LEFTY. (*Yells to* JOE.) This is a fine time for you to go nuts on me— just when we cop the title!

MAX. Which reminds me, Lefty, I get a forty percent cut on the receipts.

JOE. Max is right, Lefty. And don't call me nuts.

LEFTY. (*Unable to stand any more—weakly.*) Give me some aspirin, Doc.

(DOCTOR *hands small bottle to* LEFTY.)

MAX. Now that the case is all cleared up, Inspector ——

WILLIAMS. (*Yells.*) Sure, it's cleared up. Farnsworth is in an ice-box and Murdock is going to get into him and invite us all to his wedding—that clears it up fine! (*Savagely.*) Now, I'm going to do a little clearing up—and I'll start with you, Levene. (*He grabs* MAX, *but* JOE *rushes over and shoves* WILLIAMS *off.*)

JOE. Lay off Max, Inspector. He had nothing to do with it. It was Mrs. Farnsworth and Tony who shot me and stuck me in the ice-box!

LEFTY. (*Yells.*) Who wants to buy a screwy fighter cheap?

(JORDAN *enters from some dark corner—*JOE *looks at him.*)

JOE. Hello, Mr. Jordan—I've been waiting for you! (*All turn and look, but, of course, don't see* JORDAN. *They all stare at* JOE, *who starts pushing them all out.*) Look, fellas, scram—the whole gang of you. I got to talk private business with Mr. Jordan.

LEFTY. Take it easy, K. O., take it easy, fella!

JOE. (*Pushing them.*) Scram ——

LEFTY. We can't leave you alone in your condition.

JOE. My condition is perfect—in the pink! (*Continues pushing them*

—*angrily.*) Are you going or do I have to throw you all out? (*He gets them to door.*)

WILLIAMS. I'm not leaving here until I make head or tail out of this damn ——

LEFTY. (*Apprehensively.*) Maybe we better go, Inspector —— (*He whispers something in* WILLIAMS' *ear, which seems to please Inspector.*)

WILLIAMS. (*Smiles.*) Yeah—that's an idea. (*To* JOE, *patting him.*) All right, fella—we'll go—but don't try sneaking off with Jordan —— (*He looks lugubriously around for* JORDAN.) because I'm coming back here with a nice little present for both of you—a nice little *jacket* you'll be *crazy* about!

JOE. Aw, you don't have to give me anything, Inspector. Thanks, just the same.

WILLIAMS. Don't mention it. (*To others.*) Come on. (*They all exit; but* MAX *hangs back.* WILLIAMS *grabs him.*) You too, Levene.

MAX. Nix. *I'm in on this deal!* I gotta see that Jordan puts Joe back in Farnsworth, and ——

WILLIAMS. (*Collaring* MAX.) Yeah, I know—but first I'm going to put you into something! Come on ——

(*As he drags* MAX *out, the rest follow, casting half-frightened, half-worried looks back at* JOE, *who now turns and smiles at* JORDAN.)

JOE. I'm sure glad you're here, Mr. Jordan. Did you see the fight?

JORDAN. Yes, Joe. You did a nice job. You made Murdock very happy. He's grateful to you!

JOE. How is he?

JORDAN. Fine! Fine!

JOE. Swell.

JORDAN. You fought beautifully, cleanly, scientifically. You make it an art.

JOE. (*Beaming.*) I'm back in my old form again!

JORDAN. This is your niche, Joe—this is where you belong—where you were meant to be—world champion!

JOE. Not me—Murdock is. I'm glad I did it for him, but now *get me out of this* —— (*He squirms as if trying to shed a suit of clothes.*)

JORDAN. (*Quietly.*) Joe!

JOE. (*Looking at him.*) Yeah?

JORDAN. The Registrar couldn't do anything with Farnsworth!

JOE. (*Stunned.*) You mean I can't have him back?

JORDAN. Farnsworth is adamant.

JOE. Gee, Mr. Jordan, what's going to happen to me? And Bette?

JORDAN. You won't be cheated, Joe. Nobody is, really. Eventually all things work out—there is design in everything—in the wing of an insect; the bill of a bird; the eye of an eagle; everything has a perfect balance. It's no good grafting one tree or flower into another of a different nature—the lines of distinction are clear and the limitations inflexible. You and Murdock are one—you belong to each other—this is your life—your destiny—you're back now on your own road!

JOE. (*Angrily.*) Nix! It's no good without Bette—I don't want those sixty years if I can't have her.

JORDAN. You'll have everything that was ordained for you.

JOE. I don't care about anything else. A fellow only meets a girl like her once. Murdock is swell—I'd be proud to be him—carry on for him—keep his name clean—like he would—but I got Bette loving Farnsworth, and I gotta be him or I'll lose her. (*Determinedly.*) I got an idea! You wait here while I take a shower and I'll *go talk to Farnsworth!* I should have handled this myself right from the start —you guys fumble everything—don't go away—I'll be back in a minute. (*He hurries into the shower.*)

JORDAN. (*After him, softly.*) Goodbye—Joe! (*In a different voice, cheerily.*) Good luck, "K. O. Murdock!" (*He snaps his fingers and hurries out.*)

(*For a moment we hear the rushing noise of the shower and* JOE's *grunts as he briskly slaps himself; then* MAX, LEFTY *and* WILLIAMS *re-enter.*)

WILLIAMS. Where is he?

MAX. (*Hears shower.*) In the shower!

LEFTY. Tie that, will you. Taking a shower with a bullet in his heart!

MAX. (*Grimly.*) With that guy Jordan around, don't be surprised no matter what happens!

LEFTY. (*To* LEVENE.) Say, you're as nuts as Murdock.

WILLIAMS. Well, nuts or not, he knew what he was talking about when he told me Farnsworth was in an icebox. My man found him —frozen stiff.

MAX. (*Excitedly, to* WILLIAMS.) What did they do with the body?

WILLIAMS. It's down to the morgue.

MAX. Tell them not to touch it. *Joe needs that body!*

WILLIAMS. (*Roars.*) What for?

MAX. To get married in!

WILLIAMS. Now don't start *that* again.

MAX. I better tell Joe.

(*As he starts toward shower* JOE, *now* UNCHANGEABLY *Murdock, but, of course, looking like* JOE *to the audience, comes out—a robe over him; he seems to be in a kind of trance. Slowly, he walks toward the rubbing table.* LEFTY, WILLIAMS *and* MAX *stare worriedly at him.*)

LEFTY. (*Over to him.*) How do you feel now, K. O.?

JOE. (*Looks at* LEFTY.) Kinda funny, Lefty—kinda funny.

(WILLIAMS *and* MAX *come over to him.*)

LEFTY. I'm surprised you ain't collapsed.

(JOE *sits on table.*)

MAX. (*To* JOE.) The Inspector found Farnsworth in the icebox and took him to the morgue. You and Jordan better hustle right down there.

(JOE *stares uncomprehendingly at him.*)

WILLIAMS. Keep out of this, Levene. (*To* JOE.) You may be cuckoo as hell, Murdock, but you certainly steered me right on the Farnsworth case. I telephoned my man and he found him just as you said —and what's more, we got a confession out of Mrs. Farnsworth and her boy friend! (*Laughs.*) But you're wrong on one thing, Murdock. Farnsworth is in no condition to get married! (*He glares at* MAX.)

JOE. You fellows must have me mixed up with somebody else. I don't know any Farnsworth—and I don't remember telling you anything.

(MAX *stares worriedly at* JOE.)

WILLIAMS. Now he's lost his memory.

JOE. (*To* LEFTY.) Who's this guy, Lefty?

LEFTY. (*Sick at heart.*) He's the Police Inspector, K. O.—remember?

JOE. No. What's he want?

LEFTY. Never mind, K. O. (*Hands him clothes.*) Here—get dressed —I'm taking you to a hospital!

JOE. You out of your mind, Lefty? I got to climb in the ring in a few minutes! (*He leaps off table, flexes legs and starts shadow-boxing.*) And I'm in swell shape, too—never better. I'll chop Smallings down in one minute flat—same as I did "Puggsy" Whalen in Chicago last March—remember?

LEFTY. (*In despair.*) You *already* chopped him down, K. O.—the fight's over—you're *champ!*

JOE. (*Stares at him.*) The fight's over? (LEFTY *nods.*) And—I'm champ?

LEFTY. Sure, K. O.

JOE. (*Dazedly starts putting on clothes.*) What—what round did I get him, Lefty?

LEFTY. The second ——

JOE. (*Dressing.*) Funny—I can't remember! I can't remember anything!

LEFTY. (*Grimly.*) You remember this bullet, don't you? (*Throws open* JOE's *robe to show wound, then gulps.*) What—what happened to it?

JOE. To what?

LEFTY. The bullet—Doc said it was right in your heart!

(WILLIAMS *and* MAX *stare at* JOE's *chest and blink in astonishment.*)

JOE. You musta had one too many, Lefty!

LEFTY. But I tell you I saw it, K. O. (*Indicates* WILLIAMS *and* MAX.) They saw it, too—didn't you, fellows?

WILLIAMS. (*Gulping.*) I—I *think* I did.

LEFTY. Don't hedge—you *know* you did.

WILLIAMS. Well, it's not there now—there ain't a mark on him.

LEFTY. (*Stares at* JOE; *wide-eyed.*) Jeez—I'm scared! This never happened to me before.

MAX. (*Grimly.*) It's that guy Jordan. (*To* JOE.) Where is he, Joe?

JOE. Who's Jordan? And what are you calling me Joe for?

(MAX *gapes at him.*)

WILLIAMS. Well, if he's not shot any more, there's no use my hanging around here. Goodbye, boys. (*He exits.*)

MAX. (*Worried, approaching* JOE.) Joe—look at me—take a good look ——

JOE. (*Looks at* MAX.) What do I want to look at you for? (*He slips on trousers.*)

MAX. Don't you *know* me?

JOE. (*Dressing.*) Sure ——

MAX. Who am I?

JOE. Don't you know?

MAX. (*Grimly.*) I have my doubts. You tell me.

JOE. You're Max Levene ——

MAX. Yeah And who are you?

JOE. K.O. Murdock.

MAX. You're sure?

JOE. *(To* LEFTY.*)* What's the matter with him?

MAX. Are you anybody else besides K. O. Murdock?

JOE. *(To* LEFTY.*)* Listen to the screwball.

MAX. Do you know Joe—Joe Pendleton?

JOE. *(Slowly.)* Joe Pendleton —— *(Thinks, as* MAX *watches him anxiously.)* Oh, yeah—sure, you managed him, didn't you?

MAX. How well did you know him?

JOE. Not so well—I only met him a couple of times. Funny guy— he was always tellin' me some day he'd take my measure —— *(MAX is crestfallen.)* Say—whatever happened to him?

MAX. Don't *you* know?

JOE. I wouldn't ask you if I did, would I?

MAX. *(Slowly, as he stares at* JOE.*)* He—he—was killed—airplane crash ——

JOE. Oh, yeah—yeah, now I remember—I read something about it—tough break. He was a nice kid.

MAX. *(Gulping.)* Yeah—he sure was. *(To* LEFTY, *briskly.)* Let you and me go outside—I got a proposition for you.

LEFTY. I ain't interested, Levene.

MAX. You'll be plenty interested when I tell you.

LEFTY. *(Relunctantly.)* Well—I'll listen.

MAX. That's all I ask! *(To* JOE.*)* We'll be right back.

*(*JOE *nods,* LEFTY *and* MAX *exit.* JOE *continues dressing. After a moment door opens and* BETTE *enters.* JOE *stops dressing and they stand looking at each other a moment without recognition.)*

JOE. Hello.

BETTE. *(Timidly.)* Are you Mr. Murodck?

JOE. Yeah. That's me.

BETTE. I—I'm looking for Mr. Levene.

JOE. *(Staring at her.)* He just left.

BETTE. *(Turning to go.)* Thank you.

JOE. Wait a minute. *(*BETTE *stops, she and* JOE *look at each other, strangely drawn to each other.)* Don't—don't I know you?

BETTE. I don't think so, Mr. Murdock.

JOE. No, I guess I don't. For a minute—I—I thought maybe I did. I felt sure I'd seen you before. Funny, ain't it, how you sometimes feel you know people.

BETTE. (*Looking at him.*) Yes.

JOE. Did—did you like the fight?

BETTE. I didn't see it.

JOE. Gee—that's too bad.

BETTE. But I heard it over the radio. (*She looks curiously at him.*) Oh—your eye is hurt.

JOE. (*Staring fascinatedly at her.*) It's nothing. Just swole a little ——

BETTE. It's all red.

JOE. Aw, it don't hurt.

BETTE. Your lip is cut, too. (*She touches it tenderly with the tips of her fingers.* JOE *is thrilled.* BETTE *hastily withdraws her hand.*) I—I don't know why I did that!

JOE. It felt good. Would—would you do it again, please? (BETTE *laughs.*) Gee—you laugh beautiful, Miss—Miss ——

BETTE. Logan.

JOE. Mine's Murdock. Tom Murdock—but everybody calls me "K. O."

BETTE. (*Smiling.*) How do you do?

JOE. Hello! (*They keep staring at each other, completely fascinated.*) You interested in the fight game?

BETTE. I knew a man who was.

JOE. Yeah—who? Maybe I know him.

BETTE. Jonathan Farnsworth.

JOE. Oh, I heard something about him from the boys. Knocked off by his wife, wasn't he?

BETTE. (*Chokingly.*) Yes.

JOE. Was—was he a friend of yours?

BETTE. (*Quietly.*) I loved him.

JOE. (*Sympathetically.*) Gee—that's tough. (*Suddenly the lights go out—the stage is dark.*) Hey, put on those lights! (*To* BETTE.) Don't get scared, Miss Logan —— (*Yells.*) Hey —— (*The beam from a flashlight pierces the dark.*) Who's there?

OLD MAN. It's me, Mr. Murdock —— (*The light enters and we can distinguish the* OLD MAN *tottering in.*) The fuse blew out. I'll have it fixed in a moment. (OLD MAN *hobbles up-stage near lockers.*)

JOE. Hurry up—there's a young lady here.

OLD MAN. Right away, Mr. Murdock.

JOE. (*To* BETTE.) I'm sorry. Are you all right?

BETTE. Yes, thank you.

(*Lights come on again,* JOE *and* BETTE *look at each other—they pay no attention to the* OLD MAN, *but we now recognize him as* JORDAN. *He continues to fuss with lights.*)

JOE. (*Looking wonderingly at her.*) When—when the lights went out, I tried hard to think where I saw you. In the dark your voice sounded like—like I'd heard it before—but I couldn't remember where—or when. Did—did you feel anything, Miss Logan?

BETTE. (*Looking strangely at him.*) Yes, I did, I—I seemed to be standing high up—on a hilltop—looking down at the sea—and you were there, swimming towards the shore, looking up at me—trying to say something—shouting something—something, I felt I heard long ago—so long ago that it may have been in another existence!

JOE. (*Eagerly.*) Maybe that's it, Miss Logan. Maybe we knew each other some time, way back, maybe. Funnier things than that can happen. Anyhow, you don't seem *strange* to me—I feel I've *always* known you. We—we *couldn't* be strangers and feel like we do, could we?

BETTE. (*Softly.*) Perhaps not. (JORDAN *looks at them and smiles.*) I—I'd better be going. (*As she turns to go,* JOE *stops her.*)

JOE. (*Impulsively.*) No—please don't go. I don't know why I should feel like this, but I—I'd be awful lonesome if you left me now. I know I gotta lot of nerve, but if—if you're not doing anything—I mean if nobody is waiting for you—would you like to go get a bite with me—there's a nice little place, Mike's, just around the corner where I always go after my fights. I—I want us to get better acquainted. Will you—please, Miss Logan?

BETTE. (*Looks at him—then smiles.*) All right, Mr. Murdock. I remember now, I promised Jonathan—I mean Mr. Farnsworth—that I'd be nice to—to a certain fighter he said I'd meet soon!

JOE. (*Happily.*) Gee—then I'm in luck! Come on, Miss Logan. (*As they start out,* JOE *sees* JORDAN *for the first time now. He stares at him.*) Hey—haven't I seen you somewhere? (*To* BETTE.) Gee—I asked *you* that, too, didn't I?

(BETTE *nods.*)

JORDAN. (*Quietly, smiling.*) We've met, Mr. Murdock.

JOE. (*Staring at him.*) Sure—now I know. You're Jim Langley— used to be middle-weight champ—— (*Pats* JORDAN *on back.*) I never missed one of your scraps—I learned a lot from you.

JORDAN. I sincerely hope so.

JOE. Say—how're you fixed for money, Jim?

JORDAN. I don't need any, thank you.

JOE. Everybody needs it—here —— (*Hands* JORDAN *some bills.*) — this is my big night—I feel good—I feel great—better'n I ever felt before in my life—just like a new-born babe—the world's swell!

JORDAN. I'm delighted you feel like that, Mr. Murdock.

JOE. I'm a lucky guy, all right—guess I was born under a lucky star —Here I am, world's heavyweight champ at twenty-three—and I—I just met —— (*He looks at* BETTE; *softly.*) —her.

JORDAN. I don't like to hurry you, children, but I've got to close up. *My job is finished!* I've got to get back home.

JOE. Sure, Jim, sure. Sorry we held you up. (*To* BETTE.) Come on, Bette. Say, I got a nerve calling you Bette, ain't I?

BETTE. How did you know my first name?

JOE. You told me, didn't you?

BETTE. No. (*Pause.*) That was strange.

JOE. Pretty familiar to a girl I just met.

(BETTE *laughs.*)

JORDAN. Run along! Good luck and God bless you both.

JOE. Thanks. (*He and* BETTE *start out.*) So long, Jim.

JORDAN. So long, *K. O. Murdock!*

(BETTE *and* JOE *go out, as* JORDAN *smiles after them, and starts turning out lights.* MAX *rushes in rather excited, waves a paper in his hand.*)

JORDAN. Looking for somebody?

MAX. Yeah—Joe Pendleton, Alias K. O. Murdock, alias Farnsworth, alias God knows who! I just bought a half interest in him from Lefty. (*Sees saxophone and grabs it.*) Where'd he go?

JORDAN. (*Significantly.*) K. O. Murdock just left. *There isn't any Joe Pendleton—not any more.* Good night. (*He hobbles out as* MAX *stands there staring after him.*)

CURTAIN